LEARN EARN RETURN

The Journey of a Global Entrepreneur

BY BERT TWAALFHOVEN

WITH SHIRLEY SPENCE

APRIL 2013

Published by EFER
7 Place Flagey
1050 Brussels, Belgium
ler@efer.eu
http://www.efer.eu

ISBN 9 789082 066326 Spiral bound
ISBN 9 789082 066319 Paperback
ISBN 9 789082 066302 eBook

Contents

Foreword
by Tea Petrin

In telling the story of an entrepreneur, Bert Twaalfhoven, this book explores the entrepreneurial process, the identification and pursuit of opportunity, the growth of new ventures, and the harvesting of value created. It is not a book of tools for entrepreneurship since that cannot be. It is well recognized that entrepreneurs work in an unknown world, making it impossible to determine any rules according to which entrepreneurs would have to act. It is a book about Twaalfhoven's fascinating entrepreneurial journey throughout his life, and it offers many valuable insights into what it means to practice entrepreneurship.

Why Bert Twaalfhoven, you may ask.

It is because entrepreneurship is not only about technological leadership, it is also about improving economic welfare. From this perspective, high-tech entrepreneurs are not the only entrepreneurs contributing to economic welfare improvements, other entrepreneurs who perform the entrepreneurial function of finding solutions to existing problems also contribute. Such entrepreneurs come from all walks of life. They can be found in different technological industries, service sectors, and the public sector. Many of them can reach global markets despite not being technology leaders. I call these entrepreneurs "hidden champions" because not much is publicly known about them, yet they are indispensable to economic development. Entrepreneurs are the key generators of change, which in turn generates economic development through the creation of new combinations of already existing resources and production processes. They create something different. To study entrepreneurship means to study economic change. This study needs to embrace entrepreneurs, enterprises, structures, and changes at the industry level and the markets, society, economies, and political systems in which they operate.

By reading this book carefully, the reader will be able to get an overall perspective of what entrepreneurship is all about, i.e., the role of entrepreneurs in shaping industrial and economic change. The growth and global reach presented in this book illustrates this point. All companies that remain active in providing jobs and expanding are important generators of growth; they are Twaalfhoven's entrepreneurial legacy. They are the fruits of his entrepreneurial spirit mixed with other contextual entrepreneurial ingredients.

As a professor of entrepreneurship for more than 20 years, I am disappointed by the attitude of too many students who see entrepreneurship as a means to strike it rich. They forget that entrepreneurship is much more. It is a way of life; it is the drive to realize one's own idea. Monetary rewards come second. Entrepreneurs return to society in many ways, not just by driving economic growth. The issue of return in the entrepreneurial life story of Bert Twaalfhoven is really exceptional. Knowing Bert well for more than 13 years, I was impressed both by his economic contribution as a global entrepreneur and by his commitment to entrepreneurship, but I was equally, if not more so, impressed by how he gave back to others throughout his entrepreneurial journey and beyond. Therefore, I had no difficulty finding the right title for the book: Learn, Earn, Return. It is Bert's slogan, and reflects his way of living—learn, earn, and return, which is captured well in the book.

Although the inspiration for this book came from the concept of "return," I believe that the other two words in the title will prove to be equally valuable to scholars teaching entrepreneurship as well as to students studying this field, who constantly ask questions related to finding good business opportunities, dealing with failure, knowing when to expect success, forming networks, recognizing a good business plan, knowing the essence of entrepreneurial behavior, understanding the difference between an entrepreneur and a manager, and so forth. Finally, this book will remind other entrepreneurs of the third part of entrepreneurial equation—*return.*

Dr. Tea Petrin is a full professor at the University of Ljubljana, and a former Minister of Economy for Slovenia

Introduction:
The Phoenix

A few years ago, I shared my story with Dirk Kuin, a Dutch journalist. We started talking about symbolism.

What would capture the essence of my life journey, and my passion for entrepreneurship, on a personal and societal level? His answer: the Phoenix.

The Phoenix is a mythical creature, a bird with brightly colored plumage that dies in a fire of its own making, only to rise again from the ashes. The Greeks called it Bennu, meaning "to rise brilliantly." Christians saw it as a metaphor for resurrection. In Russia, it is the subject of the famous ballet by Igor Stravinsky. More recently, it appears as a theme in the Harry Potter series. Cities from Beirut, Lebanon to Phoenix, Arizona use it in their emblems, to signify destruction and rebuilding. The Belgians used it on a coin commemorating Europe's rebirth from the ashes of WWII.

The Phoenix is a truly international image of enduring hope, renewal, and redemption. To me, it also signifies two inter-related and important themes in my story: crisis and opportunity.

Crisis and opportunity

I have suffered my share of catastrophes, some quite literally associated with fire. My childhood home in Holland was bombed at the end of WWII, destroying the comfortable life that our family enjoyed. That crisis, however, spurred me to obtain a scholarship for university studies in the United States, opening up a whole new world to me.

My first entrepreneurial venture, in Holland, was a complete failure. But, through it, I identified a new business opportunity that was a great success... until my factory burnt to the ground. (There's that fire again!) We rallied, though, and were up and running in five days. Welcome to entrepreneurship: opportunity and challenge; risk and reward!

Entrepreneurship does not just benefit the entrepreneur. It is an engine of economic growth. You are providing a product or service that meets a market need, and you are creating jobs in the process. *The Economist* places the blame for Europe's growth crisis squarely on a failure to encourage ambitious entrepreneurs.[1] (There is ample research to support that assertion.)

I am confident that today's - and tomorrow's – entrepreneurs will rise to the challenge.

I hope to inspire just that, in part by bringing a dose of reality to the notion of what an entrepreneur is and isn't. LER is a case study of one entrepreneur's journey.

What is an entrepreneur?

An entrepreneur is someone who pursues opportunities beyond the resources currently controlled.

That now widely accepted definition of entrepreneurship was coined by Howard Stevenson, the founding father of Harvard Business School's entrepreneurial management program, as well as a friend and a great supporter of my and others' efforts to promote entrepreneurship in Europe.

Stevenson's definition captures the essence of what an entrepreneur does beautifully. The one thing I would add is that an entrepreneur is excited by growth opportunities. SMEs (small and medium sized enterprises) and entrepreneurship are often confused, which is why I will be using use the term *dynamic entrepreneurship*.

To quote *The Economist* again, "Europe produces plenty of corner shops, hairdressers and so on. What it doesn't produce enough of is innovative companies

---

[1] Les Miserables, The Economist, July 28, 2012.

that grow quickly and end up big."[2] There is nothing wrong with establishing and operating a small business, of course. It just is a different type of endeavor than what I am talking about.

Europe needs more of what David Birch, a ground breaking Massachusetts Institute of Technology researcher, calls gazelles: growth oriented enterprises that create jobs.

Stevenson maintains that his entrepreneurship definition is applicable beyond business; you can take an entrepreneurial approach to your life. I call that entrepreneurial spirit. It's about being proactive, and looking for ways to fulfill your needs, wants, and dreams. It's about a determination to make your own way in life, whether surviving adversity, finding a job, or starting your own business.

I have been called a born entrepreneur, but take exception to that, because I don't believe that entrepreneurs are "born." Entrepreneurship can be learned (and taught), and entrepreneurs come in all sizes and shapes and nationalities. That said, most successful entrepreneurs do share some common characteristics.

Entrepreneurs are opportunity-driven. We are always looking for new things. We aren't interested in following the system. We want to create something better, more interesting, more useful. We will throw ourselves into the pursuit of an opportunity. Often, just one will not do; we'll see and want that next opportunity, too. That requires energy as well as vision, and a longer term perspective.

Entrepreneurs – good ones, at least – are not reckless gamblers. We are decisive, yes. Opportunities often are fleeting; wait too long and the "window" will close. Decisions need to be made quickly. Then you have to be ready to switch course as needed. No one wants to be wrong, but you can't be scared about it. If you misstep or even fail, try to learn from it, and move on.

Entrepreneurship is about risk and reward. So, yes, entrepreneurs are risk takers,

[2] Les Miserables, The Economist, July 28, 2012.

but we take calculated risks. Sometimes "calculated" may mean worry and re-evaluate, because creating something new often means treading uncharted waters. It's more about managing the risk involved in a venture, ideally by getting someone to share it with you.

Entrepreneurs value independence, the freedom to do what we want – win or lose. We like to be in control, and aren't afraid to take responsibility for ourselves and others. "The buck stops here" is an exciting but demanding reality. There will be crises and setbacks, but they can be overcome. You can't do it alone, of course. You need great people around you.

Today's – and tomorrow's – entrepreneurs recognize that they are operating in a global context. They look beyond their own boundaries, and take full advantage of a global explosion of knowledge and technology. Entrepreneurship isn't just about creating something totally new. It's also about seeing something in one place that can meet a need somewhere else, and seizing the opportunity.

Hopefully, you now have a clearer picture of the subject of this book: a dynamic entrepreneur. Now, let me tell you more about why I have written it, and what you can expect from taking the time to read it.

About this book

I am a proud champion of entrepreneurship in Europe. That is the reason for this book.

My main vehicle for promoting entrepreneurship over the past 25 years has been the European Forum for Entrepreneurial Research (EFER), which I co-founded in 1987. One day, in Brussels, the EFER team was discussing an upcoming colloquium. The discussion turned to lingering misperceptions about entrepreneurs as fixated on getting rich quick, with little if any sense of responsibility to the profession or society.

"We need the story of an entrepreneur who has achieved business success and given back," proclaimed Tea Petrin, a University of Ljubljana professor and former

Minister of Economy in Slovenia, as well as an EFER Academic Advisor. She turned in my direction, finishing her thought: "And we have one right here!"

I have a horror of ego books by self-proclaimed stars, but agreed to think about it.

I decided that it would make sense as a case study, not a lecture on the right or wrong way to be an entrepreneur. The reader would be left to make his own interpretations, and decide what might apply to his or her particular situation.

There has been lots of activity, since then, to distil decades' worth of life and career experience. In my usual fashion, I have sought and incorporated many ideas about what would be most useful. And, here is where we have ended up, with LEARN EARN RETURN (LER).

The purpose of this book is to share, with all who might be interested, what I have learned about being a global entrepreneur. It is not a recipe for instant success; my story is filled with failures. But I believe that we learn from our own and others' experiences, and am happy to share mine with you.

My primary goal is to offer a tool that EFER and other entrepreneurship professors can use with their students, to help cultivate knowledge and skills. But equally, if not more importantly, I also hope that it will inspire students to feel that they can take destiny in their own hands by becoming entrepreneurs; that there is a viable and exciting alternative to waiting for the increasingly unlikely prospect of being handed a government or big-business job.

LER also may be of value to practicing entrepreneurs, especially European university graduates, to enhance their own success, and inspire them to give back – of their time, talent and networks as well as money – to the next generation of entrepreneurial talent, and to their communities.

Finally, I hope that the many people who are part of my story - including my fellow HBS alumni, my Indivers and EFER colleagues, the many people who have taught and inspired me, and my friends and family – will find something of interest or use in its telling. Although they might, could, and should sometimes disagree!

How to accomplish all that, in one small book?

The contents of the book draw on the over 260 talks about entrepreneurship that I have given at 62 universities in 23 countries, and many other venues. There are lots of stories, and some photos from my collection of thousands. And, because I wanted more than just my voice to be heard, you will find excerpts from interviews conducted with colleagues, friends, and family.

The structure of the book reflects my desire to go beyond a technical list of how-to's, or do's and don'ts of entrepreneurship. Some readers may choose to read it straight though. The structure also allows you to jump to topics of particular interest to you at the moment, or come back to them later.

Chapters 1 and 2 set the stage, describing my and Indivers' "life stories." Chapters 3 through 7 present five major lessons or themes, based on that experience. More specifically:

- **Chapter 1, My entrepreneurial journey: Learn, earn, and return** describes my personal journey as a career entrepreneur, and can satisfy your curiosity about how someone becomes an entrepreneur, and what an entrepreneurial life looks and feels like.

- **Chapter 2, The Indivers story: Dynamic growth** describes the 40-year evolution of a diversified multinational enterprise that achieved 15% revenue growth and 16% return on equity, from its first venture to its final major exit, in a €120 million ($162 million) deal.

- **Chapter 3, Pursuing opportunities: Getting in and getting out** begins with a general discussion of niches, and then presents four key elements of Indivers' opportunistic approach: technology spin-offs, industry analysis, going beyond your borders, and exits.

- **Chapter 4, Taking risks: Failing forward** summarizes Indivers' 16 failures, and presents four case studies: Aluminium Extruders Holland (squeezed out), QI-

Tech China (double jeopardy), Interturbine Paton (betting on the future), and North Atlantic Associates (out of control).

- **Chapter 5, *Marshalling resources: The power of networking*** talks about why and how entrepreneurs network, and describes Indivers' networks of researchers, university students, managers and board members, and financial and joint venture partners.

- **Chapter 6, *Managing growth: Professional intrapreneurship*** describes the key elements of Indivers' management philosophy and practices, including structure, people and culture, planning, controls, and crisis management.

- **Chapter 7, *Giving back: Easy, satisfying, and a responsibility*** shares my personal experience giving back to my alma maters and my profession (including the founding of EFER, the European Forum for Entrepreneurship Research); and explains why I find it so rewarding.

The Conclusion, *A call to action*, brings us full circle to the Phoenix by challenging all of us to make entrepreneurship a powerful source of personal satisfaction and societal benefit. It asks students to consider what role entrepreneurship might play in their careers and lives. It also invites institutions and individuals to support the advancement of entrepreneurship and entrepreneurs.

Now, let's get started!

A word about numbers

What's a business book without numbers?! The challenge here is that the Indivers story spans four decades. Early numbers were reported in Guilders and Dollars, and later in Euros and Dollars. We have tried our best, on the following pages, to give the most representative accounting of figures, for the time period being discussed.

CHAPTER 1

My entrepreneurial journey:

Learn, earn, and return

The book's title was coined by Tea Petrin and Dirk Kuin to describe three parts of my entrepreneurial journey. They are not chronological stages, however, so much as interwoven themes:

- Building knowledge and skills through formal education, hands-on experience, collaboration with others, and an insatiable curiosity *(learn)*
- Combining those capabilities with passion and hard work, to pursue and profit from entrepreneurial opportunities, for myself and others *(earn)*
- Recognizing those who have helped me along the way and returning the favours; and giving back to education, business, and the broader community *(return)*

My journey begins in Holland, takes me to North America for school, and brings me back to Europe to pursue my dream of being an entrepreneur. The rest of this chapter describes that journey.

Family roots

I was born in the Netherlands, in 1929, just as the world was plunged into the Great Depression, and the Nazis were coming to power in Germany.

My parents had both studied medicine, and opened a practice in The Hague, in 1925. My father was the physician, and my mother helped with medical administration, as well as taking care of me and my four sisters and two brothers.

The medical practice helped us weather the Depression in relative comfort, but exposed us to the suffering of the many less fortunate than us. We lived next to a very poor area, and there often were patients who could not pay. They were not turned away.

Many of my values are grounded in my upbringing, which included a Roman Catholic education. Discipline, perseverance, and hard work were important. My morning routine was: church at 7 am, swimming at 7:45, and then school. (I was not the best student, and had to repeat my first year of high school. But, I went on to earn my high school diploma, in 1948.)

Another value that has stuck with me is that of giving back. I remember a sermon by a pastor about "redde rationem", heard when I was young. Roughly translated, it means "Give an account of your day, your year, what you're doing with your life."

The point is that we all have talents - energy, finances, and so on – and we need to be asking ourselves: "How am I using my talents to give back to the community?" My father's service to the poor was a great example of that.

My family's life changed dramatically with WWII. Food became scarce. When survival is at stake, you become very entrepreneurial. I sold potatoes at school during the Hunger Winter, cut trees on our street, and pulled strings down the field at greyhound races. In hindsight, it was positive shock treatment, coming from a protected family.

Our high school sent us to farms in eastern Holland, first for summers, and then for the last year of the war. (I loved it and wanted to be a farmer; more on that later.) In April 1945, our neighbourhood in The Hague was accidentally bombed by Allied Forces, and my mother seriously wounded. My family lost everything, and was dispersed for over a year.

I knew that my father could not afford to send me to university, but was determined to find a way. My application for a Fulbright scholarship to study in the U.S. was rejected, but Fordham University in New York City accepted me with a one-year grant. I left Holland on the SS Volendam, with $20 in pocket money, and a job as a waiter on the ship.

That, by the way, is a powerful lesson in self-reliance!

International education

Fordham

Fordham was a life-changing experience, for a Dutch boy who had never been out of Holland. Here I was, living in the US and studying in English, part of an international student body. Fordham required visits by a formal guardian and my family did not have the money to come, but one of my father's patients - Mr. Brenninkmeijer - came to see me every month. (His family's international clothing store business included outlets in New York.)

During the school year, I worked as a dishwasher and waiter. When summer came, I hitchhiked to California, stopping on the way to pick fruit with Mexican workers, and got a job in a vineyard in San Jose. Then, my employer went bankrupt, leaving me jobless for three weeks. I contacted my father in desperation. He wired $100 - all he could spare, at the time – which allowed me to purchase a union membership, for a night shift job at the Del Monte Cannery.

Fortunately, Fordham came through with a scholarship for my remaining three years of university.

I continued to work part-time during the school year - waiter, infirmary assistant, Dutch-English translator, Coca-Cola machine fill-ups at stores and movies theatres, door to door salesman – and was a camp counsellor in Maine during the summers. I got involved with recruiting restaurant workers to join a union, for equal pay rights.

There was still time for my studies, though, and extracurricular activities such as the Industrial Club and the International Club, and playing tennis and soccer.

During my senior year, I decided to apply to Harvard Business School. Once again, luck was with me: an acceptance to the MBA Program, with a two-year scholarship loan.

Harvard Business School

The first months were tough: hours of reading, written analyses of cases, and high-intensity class discussions. But I was learning so much, from my professors and from my classmates, who were from all over the world, with experience in all sorts of businesses.

Many would go on to make their marks in the private and public sectors: John McDonald, founder of McKinsey Germany; Bill McGowan, founder of MCI; Bill Draper, one of Silicon Valley's first venture capitalists; Nick Brady, US Treasurer; Peter Lockheed, Governor of Alberta, Canada; Peter Brooke, founder of Advent; Gerry Andlinger, founder of Adlinger Associates; and Coleman Mockler, CEO of Gillette, to name just a few.

I had some outstanding professors at HBS, including Jack Glover, for Management Controls[3]; Charlie Bliss, for Accounting and Control; Charlie Williams, for Finance; Jack McLean, for Competitive Analysis and Industry Structure; and Georges Doriot, for Manufacturing. (Doriot, who also founded one of the first venture capital firms, will reappear several times in my story.)

HBS taught me fundamental business concepts and skills, and exposed me to the workings of both small and big businesses, in a wide variety of industry settings. The image of the entrepreneur appealed to me: running your own business, being your own boss, and seeing and pursuing opportunities.

We read a case about Textron and its diversification. To get out of the dying textile industry, it went into aluminium extrusions and a number of other sectors. I wrote my MBA thesis, with six classmates, on industrial diversification. When the time came, later, to name my company, Textron would serve as my inspiration.

I took full advantage of out-of-class opportunities to interact with my classmates,

---

[3] Glover's book "Attack on Big Business," which was a critique of big corporations, made quite an impact on me.

joining the Marketing, International, and European clubs; and having lots of fun as Social Chairman of the Class of 1954. There were opportunities to hone my speech-making skills, too, giving talks at Doriot's firm (American Research and Development Corporation, or ARD) and colleges in Boston, New York and New Jersey.

And, what's life without a little romance?!

One Saturday evening during my sophomore year at Fordham, I attended a dance at nearby Marymount College. That's where I met Maria Somary, a Marymount freshman. Maria's family was from Switzerland, and had moved to Washington, DC when WWII broke out. We began dating seriously my senior year at Fordham. Maria visited me at HBS from time to time, staying at the homes of professors.

During my second year at HBS, I hitchhiked to Washington DC to propose to Maria, and meet her famous father, Felix Somary. A successful banker and university professor, he also was an advisor to the U.S. Department of Defence on financial matters.

Happily, Maria said "yes," and her father liked me. In 1954, Maria and I were married in Zurich.

Now, back to business. I was graduating HBS, and needed a job.

It was the McCarthy era in the U.S. Foreigners were viewed with some suspicion, which meant that getting a work permit for the U.S. was unlikely. I got a job offer from Dutch Shell in Holland; it paid $250 per month. The Aluminium Company of Canada (Alcan) in Montreal also made an offer, at a starting salary of $350 per month.

Canada, it would be!

Although my student days were officially over, I consider my Alcan experience part of my international education, and another steppingstone to entrepreneurship.

Alcan, my first job

Alcan was one of the world's largest aluminium producers. It was fully integrated with bauxite mines, alumina refineries, smelting facilities, power generation installations, a transportation network, and some product manufacturing. It had over 120 subsidiaries worldwide.[4]

I started in the finance department, as a lowly cost accountant. We were doing price changes with a slide rule; it was awful. The CFO, an HBS graduate, rescued me, putting me on more interesting projects (e.g., consolidation of subsidiary results, and comparison of actual performance versus quarterly plan).

One day, the CFO came to us and said: "Our Ghana bauxite plant may lose several hundred million dollars. What is the impact on our subsidiaries and their cash flows, and Alcan's five-year investment plan?" We worked three days and nights to come up with new quarterly and long term plans, for Alcan's board.

Meanwhile, Maria and I were enjoying life in Montreal, and beginning our family. She taught French in an English speaking school until becoming pregnant with our first child, Bob, who was born in 1955. He was joined by Felix in 1956. We bought our first house. I served as scoutmaster for a local Boy Scout troop, and was invited to teach cases at the University of Montreal.

There also was an opportunity – somewhat accidentally – for me to fulfil my dream of being a farmer. Maria and I wanted to help a large Dutch family immigrate to Canada. At the suggestion of Canadian officials, we bought a dairy farm in southern Quebec for them to run. Of course, I could not stay out of it!

The farm's breeding practices were outdated, and milk production was poor. A specialist from Europe's top agricultural school advised us to use artificial insemination methods. It took five years, but we increased milk production by 100%, and

---

[4] In 2007, Alcan was purchased by Australian/European multinational Rio Tinto for $38 billion, becoming Rio Tinto Alcan Inc.

became a role model for French Canadian dairy farms.

At Alcan, I was learning a lot, but was frustrated. My dream was to run my own business.

Every Wednesday, the Financial Post newspaper published advertisements for new business opportunities. A few of us (me and some other HBS MBAs working at Alcan) would huddle in corners to discuss them – funeral caskets, Army condoms for export to Africa, you name it. I also was getting an idea, from an Alcan business proposal assigned to me.

The proposal was for an aluminium extrusion factory in Vancouver, Canada. (Extrusion is a process where heated aluminium blocks are pushed by a hydraulic press through a mould-die, to produce various shapes suited to specific purposes for the building industry and other customers.)

An idea came to me: why not start a factory in Holland? Entry barriers were low, and the government was offering considerable help to new businesses. The market potential for aluminium ladders and windows in Europe was good; and someone would have to do the extrusions.

In 1957, Maria's father died, and we inherited $400,000. That was a lot of money in those days, and a trigger to act on my dream of being independent. (There was a young family to take care of, though, so a substantial amount would be set aside as a cushion.) I resigned from Alcan, and began looking for a partner to start the aluminium extrusion business.[5]

There was a detour on the way to Holland, however.

When I told Professor Doriot of my plans, he said "But you don't know anything about setting up a new business." At his suggestion, I took a position at Ladenberg Thalmann, a boutique investment bank on Wall Street in New York City, while

---

[5] I have been asked "What if you hadn't inherited the money? Would you have become an entrepreneur?" My answer is that I believe I would have found a way to make it happen.

CHAPTER 1

continuing my search for partners for the Holland venture.

I left for New York, while Maria stayed in Montreal, to sell the house. The house sold, we packed the kids into a station wagon, and headed to an apartment on Long Island. Our third son, John, was born there in 1958.

By the end of the year, I had found a partner for my first entrepreneurial venture: Aluminium Extruders Holland. I was 29 years old, with no grand vision, just the desire to be my own boss, and earn a living for my family. Maria, the three boys and I boarded the New Amsterdam and set sail for Amsterdam.

> *Those were adventurous times. There was the feeling that the world was waiting for us with open arms. Europe was rebuilding, after the war. We could prove ourselves.*
>
> *- Maria Twaalfhoven*

Entrepreneurship and life

When we arrived in Holland, we settled into a rented house near Amsterdam. A bank offered me a small office in its downtown Amsterdam building, on the condition that we deposit Maria's inheritance with them.

Within three years, I would experience my first business failure and success. Our family would grow by three, with the arrival of our first daughter (Miriam, in 1959) and two more sons (Mark in 1960, and Ted in 1961). The arrivals of Wim Paul (1964) and Anne (1967) would complete the family. We would buy a home and become involved in a community outside of Amsterdam, where Maria and I still live.

Over time, Indivers would grow into a multinational enterprise, a collection of companies focused on niche opportunities. It was a roller coaster ride: 65 companies in 14 countries, including 32 start-ups, 12 acquisitions, 25 joint ventures, 35 exits, and – yes – 16 failures.

> *There's never a dull moment with Bert. He's always on the go. He's not one to give up easily, either. I've never known him to be totally down and out. If something doesn't succeed, he looks for other ways. We've had some big ups and downs, but we've been lucky with our children and, now, our grandchildren.*
>
> *- Maria Twaalfhoven*

Being an entrepreneur – especially of a fast-growing and far flung business - is not for the faint of heart. I travelled 120 days a year, on average. It's hard work, and not a nine-to-five kind of job. Crises will happen more than you'd like, at inconvenient times, and need immediate attention. As the owner, ultimately, you are responsible.

It's easy to get totally consumed by work, but that is not the solution.

Family, friends, community, and recreational activities - all help counteract the stresses of entrepreneurship. For me, family has been the most important balancer. Maria created a wonderful home for me and our eight children. Coming home, especially when the children were young, immediately took my mind off business.

We like to say that the Twaalfhovens are a truly international family. Maria and I wanted our kids to have the same opportunity for an international education that we had. Collectively, they studied at 13 different universities, in six different countries. All of them earned bachelor's degrees, five went on to earn MBA degrees, and three are engineers.

When the children were young, we would take two weeks of vacation as a family, including Christmas ski holidays and visits with Maria's family in Switzerland. Maria and I were involved with their schools, and we all attended church each Sunday. The kids are grown now, of course, but we try to stay in touch. And, there are 22 grandchildren to enjoy!

Hobbies are great stress relievers, for me. I have many, but sailing is my great love. My sailboat is docked just twenty minutes from my home. Some especially stressful days, I would leave work at 3 or 4 pm, and go to the boat. Taking care of the sails, the wind, and the storms was my way of recuperating; tremendously relaxing.

Maria may have put it best: "When you're trying to attain something, you have to be able to let go, sometimes."

Transition and legacy

Someone asked me, not that long ago: "Bert, why don't you retire?!"

Well, I have – twice!

Around Christmas 1999, I decided to retire as President of Indivers. Recuperating from the shingles, I knew that I could leave the business in the capable hands of our CEO and our international Board of Directors. At the time, our major subsidiary, Interturbine, was examining acquisitions to fit in with a new growth strategy.

But, early in 2000, everything changed.

Interturbine's board and managers felt it was the right time to sell the business, which brought me back into the thick of things. In 2001, we accepted an offer of €120 million, which ultimately translated to $162 million

I retired (again) formally in 2003.

How does it feel to realize that something you have spent a career building has passed out of your hands?

For me, it was a gradual thing, a slow pulling back from my chairman, coaching and operational roles, beginning in the mid-1990s. It felt like a reawakening, as my focus shifted from Indivers to EFER. As I was saying "good bye" to Indivers, we were staging EFER's first Colloquium for European Professors of Entrepreneurship!

Many of the companies that we built at Indivers are still in business, providing jobs and creating customer and economic value. A number of Indivers managers became entrepreneurs themselves, and many students worked and learned with us. In that sense, Indivers lives on.

My proudest entrepreneurial legacy, though, may be my efforts to promote the profession, especially through EFER.

The founding of EFER in 1987 seemed the logical extension of my efforts, since the late 1970s, to increase the awareness, understanding, and practice of entrepreneurship in Europe. It is, for me, about giving back to the field that has been so satisfying and rewarding to me personally, and holds such great potential for Europe's future. (We'll be talking much more about EFER in Chapter 7.)

For now, suffice it to say that one benefit of "retirement" (my life seems as busy as ever!) is having more time to advance EFER's cause and work, and enjoy my large and still growing family.

Hopefully, this chapter has provided a context for what follows: a closer look at my pursuit of entrepreneurial opportunities, through Indivers.

Bert
(in front) and four of his six brothers and sisters.

Neightbourhood of the Twaalfhoven family home in The Hague , accendentallly bombed during WWII

Bert set sail on the SS Volendam for Fordham University with $20 in his pocket.

Fordham soccer team (Bert standing in the center)

Fordham University New York City

Bert
in the Rocky Mountains, on his way to
California for the summer.

Professor Joe Fitzpatrick SJ,
who taught sociology, was an
important influence.

Bert and his future wife, Maria Somary, at his Fordham graduation.

Harvard Business School Boston, MA

Professor George Doriot, Manufacturing

Professor Charlie Williams, Finance

Professor Jack McLean, Competitive
Analysis and Industry Structure

Bert
on his way to Montreal, Quebec, to work for
Alcan Canada.

Bert at the Quebec farm he bought for a Dutch im-
migrant farmer to run (with the farmer's son).

Bert's first son, Felix, and Maria's
father, Felix Somary.

Bert and his three children, sailing to Holland in
1959. (Maria took the picture.)

A Twaalfhoven family vacation in 1974,
rafting on the Colorado River.

Bert and Aad van Noord (Indivers CFO) taking
a break on a business trip to Las Vegas.

Bert slalom skiing at the World Economic
Forum in Davos, Switzerland, 1984.

Sail on! Bert's life philosophy and passion.

The Indivers story:

Dynamic growth

"How did you that?!"

That is the question that typically is asked, when I show this mapping of Indivers' forty year history.

Figure 2-1 Indivers' Evolution

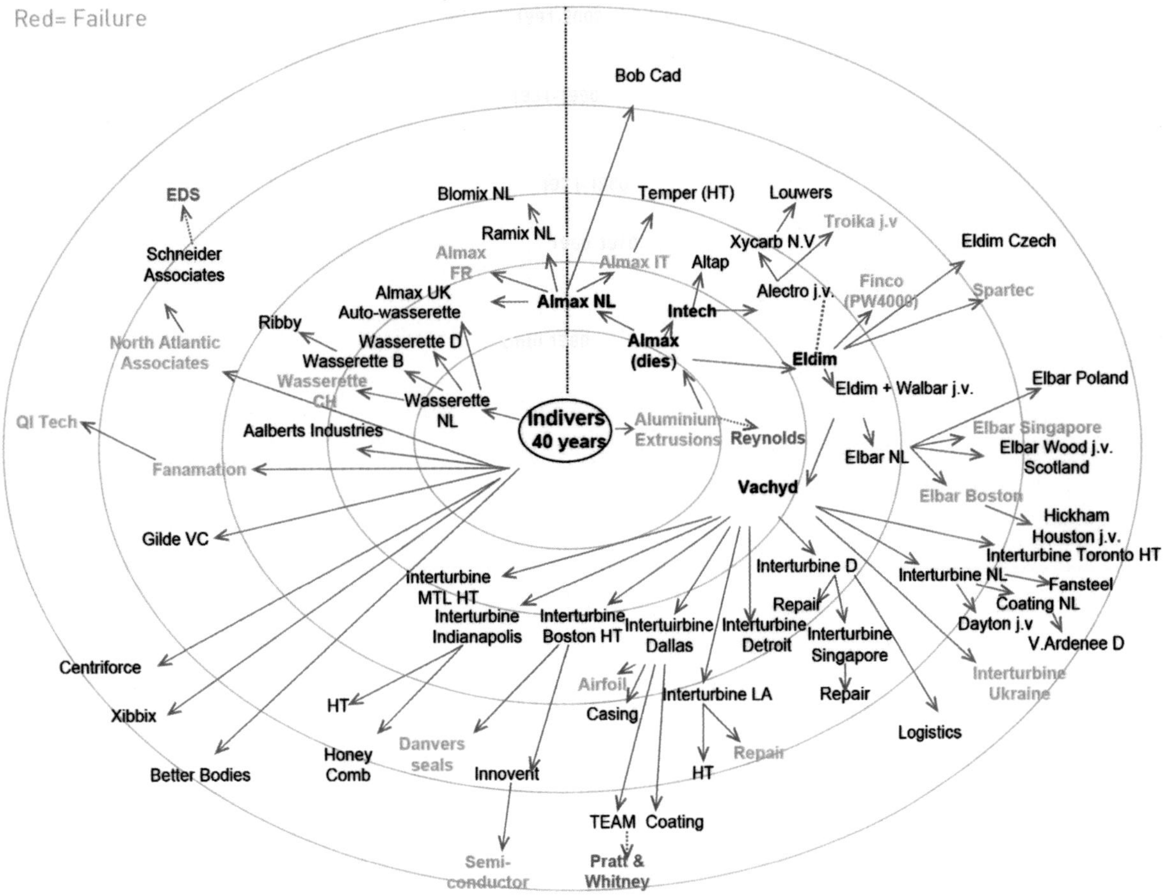

The chart was produced as part of a study being conducted by the Centre for Entrepreneurial Learning (part of the Judge Business School at the University of Cambridge).

The researchers depicted the creation and disposition of Indivers' companies as a "family" of concentric circles, representing four decades of activity. The blue arrows show the relationships among the various companies. Failures are flagged in red, and exits in green.

I like it, because it captures the complexity of a dynamic growth company.

Indivers, you could say, was built by exploiting small niches, and expanding into international markets. That sounds neat and tidy, doesn't it? But, as a friend and colleague reminded me (with a smile): "It was more like a bar room brawl." There were more than 40 start-ups, 12 acquisitions, 20 joint ventures, a dozen spinoffs, and 25 sales.

Over forty years, Indivers operated more than 65 companies in 14 countries, offering products and services in three broad technology segments: laundry, tooling, and turbine. We also experimented with a few other ventures. (See Exhibit 2-1 for a summary list of companies, by segment.)

What was Indivers, then: a business, or a collection of niches?

Bert found markets, and addressed needs. At first, he seemed to be all over the place, from washing machine services to aluminium manufacturing. In time, the seemingly "random" identification of opportunities evolved into a strategic vision; He did a study to map out the entire jet engine supply chain, and asked: "How can I plug the gaps?" As his companies evolved, Bert was never afraid to close or sell a business, or buy one. Entrepreneurship isn't just about starting from scratch. Nor is it about blind passion – there is a strong element of cool headedness that Bert exhibited.

- Daniel Isenberg

I would describe it as a portfolio of companies, and myself as a portfolio entrepreneur. Indivers was established as a holding company, with Textron as my model. The lesson from that HBS case study, for me, was that one sector can compensate for another; as one declines, you send resources in a new direction. Indivers, as the name implied, was about INdustrial DIVERSification.

Indivers – ultimately – is a success story. Over forty years, we achieved a growth rate of over 15% in revenues, and earned a 16% compound return on our equity, on average. In 2001, we sold Interturbine (our major asset) for €120 million, which became $162 million.

That said, there are failures along the way, 16 of them. The learnings presented in Chapters 3 through 7 reflect all of those experiences.

This chapter will set the stage, by presenting Indivers' "life story" in four parts: my first failure, Aluminium Extruders; my first success, Wasserette; the tooling ventures that sprang from my aluminium extrusion failure; and the turbine component business that evolved from tooling.

My first failure, Aluminium Extruders

Aluminium extrusion was the reason for returning to Holland. But, what looked like a good opportunity was short-lived: joint venture formation in 1959; start-up in 1960; production delays due to technical problems; and my expulsion as CEO and minority partner in 1961.

I then spent two years in a lawsuit to recoup my investment. (For a more detailed account of the story, see Chapter 4.)

The positive spin is that the aluminium extrusion failure would reveal another, better opportunity!

My first success, Wasserette

Aluminium Extruders' production delays meant no revenues, which presented me with a very immediate problem: I needed to find a way to make some money! (I had a young family to support, you'll recall.)

One day, a man from Surinam came to my office, selling coin-operated radios. I bought 40 of them, for $6,000, and convinced the Hotel Schiller in Amsterdam to put them in their guest rooms. Every Friday, I got the room key, to collect coins from the radios.

An idea clicked: coin-operated washing machines! At HBS, I had serviced washing machines in campus dormitories, as one of my part-time jobs. In Continental Europe, it would be a new phenomenon.

I decided to invest $20,000 to import 12 washing machines from the U.S., and start a franchise laundry business. Finding good locations (i.e., central to apartment buildings) would be essential, but no retail licenses would be required, as was the case for other kinds of stores.

But first, what to call it?

An advertising agency in Amsterdam came up with 12 names that were tested with 100 people. The winner was Wasserette. I registered it immediately. Two days later, the washing machine manufacturer tried to trademark the service, but it was too late. The Wasserette brand would prove valuable, and had to be defended more than once.[6]

I opened the first Wasserette in Amsterdam, hiring Elly Koot (a former Miss Holland) and her mother as attendants. It was tremendously successful, even featured in a Dutch newspaper article as "a U.S. invention."

The next Saturday, I ran an ad in the same newspaper that said "If you want to

---

[6] One interesting case: the popular Dutch singer Adele Bloemendaal's song "Yvette in the Wasserette." The Dutch dictionary also had to be reprinted, to include the Wasserette name.

own your own business, come to BT." It generated 150 responses. The timing was perfect, because a large number of European nationals were returning home from Indonesia and North America, eager to invest in a business. (Several of them, not altogether by chance, were HBS alumni.)

It was already clear to me that franchising would not work; laundries were an owner-operator kind of business. New approach: Wasserette would find the location (and guarantee no competition within a certain distance), buy and install the equipment, and allow the use of our name. The buyer would pay us a one-time fee for our services, on top of the start-up expenses.

Our Wasserette team sold more than 200 stores in Holland, which were built and installed over several years. We also expanded to Germany, Belgium, and Switzerland, and would ultimately sell and install more than 350 Wasserette laundries. I had my first success!

There were some bumps along the way, however. Each new country presented new challenges, we discovered. The Germans liked steam; we piped it in. Problem solved. The Swiss insisted on very hot water; we increased the temperature, but that caused the clothes to shrink. No solution; the laundry closed.

We looked at some related opportunities, too. Dry cleaning was popular in the U.S., sometimes co-located with a laundry. We opened one, and soon closed it; the chemical fumes were dangerous, and the cost of fixing the problem was prohibitive.

How about car washes, another U.S. innovation? We could play on our brand by calling them "Autowasserettes." We imported the equipment, and had a successful launch in Holland. But, when we expanded to Belgium, complaints came pouring in about car lacquer being stripped off. The problem: different car models, with different tolerances for high water pressure. We closed down.

In 1968, the laundry business was still thriving, but my attention was turning to what I saw as better growth opportunities, in tooling. We sold the Wasserette enterprise (i.e., brand name, and Bendix washing machine import for Holland, Germany, and Belgium) for a few million dollars. The exit timing was good: Wasserette's success attracted a wave of competitors from the U.S.

Tooling ventures

One of the problems we encountered at Aluminium Extruders was that dies used in the extrusion process had to be imported weekly from the U.S., causing costly delays. In 1963, an Australian colleague had the idea of making the tools in Holland.

We recruited two English engineers and a Dutch technician to help us launch Almax, setting up a plant to make moulds and dies for local customers. The investment of $75,000 paid off handsomely. Almax enjoyed a virtual monopoly, attracting customers from all over Europe. Because fast delivery is a key success factor, we opened Almax factories in Italy, France and the UK.

The tooling business grew through a series of technology spin-offs, including the production of dies and moulds for other applications (e.g., plastic bottles and pipes), and support for tool manufacturers (e.g., heat treatment, and CAD/CAM systems). (See Chapter 3, for more details) Local customers were served by small shops, each focused on a specialized technology.

Turbine components

In 1966, a fire at the Almax Holland plant - caused by a spark erosion machine - led to the discovery that spark erosion also had jet engine applications. We did an industry study, and saw huge potential for small suppliers of jet engine components and processes, on a global scale. Eldim was our first foray into the jet engine market, in 1970. (See Chapter 3)

In 1974, we acquired VacHyd, a U.S.-based chain of heat treatment companies.

We initially saw it as a service for tool manufacturers. When it turned out that it also worked on jet engines, VacHyd became the core of our turbine business. That year, we set up Interturbine as a separate holding company, to house VacHyd and other turbine companies.

By 1987, it was clear that Indivers' major growth opportunities were in turbine, including large, stationary engines (for industrial applications, such as power generation and gas transport), and flying engines (for commercial and military aircraft). To pursue them, we would need capital.

We began selling smaller tooling companies, and made what would be the first of three major, strategic exits by Indivers: the sale of our Intech Division, which was profitable but engaged in what we now considered side activities (e.g., graphite sourcing and tooling).

We intended to offer Intech on the London Stock Exchange (LSE), but opted out when the market soured due to a recession. Gerald Carter, Intech's CEO (and IN-SEAD alumnus), proposed a management buyout, and lined up some venture capitalists and a bank. We sold Intech to them for $20 million.

In 1982, the European Management Forum (which later became the World Economic Forum) named Indivers one of its Top 100 Pioneer Enterprises. Exhibit 2-2 shows why. Over the 1964-1986 period, our total revenues grew from $4 million to $80 million. Our continuing revenues (i.e., excluding Intech) would be $60 million.

Our growth strategy for Interturbine was to target specific manufacturing, repair, and metallurgical process niches. By the 1990s, we were operating 15 facilities, including four focused on stationary engines (the Elbar "family"), and eleven supporting flying turbines (the Eldim side).

The aviation side of the business, we had quickly learned, was a complex game with big players, but we were able to secure our little spots in its massive supply chain.

Interturbine held FAA[7] and most other country aviation authority approvals to repair the world's leading aircraft engines, and served 67 airlines and most top overhaul shops. We were investing in the future, by partnering with Pratt & Whitney (P&W) on the development of its next generation engine, and forming a joint venture to develop a new, high-tech ceramic coating process.

However, the capital investment and research and development spending required to stay competitive was beginning to take its toll. In 1996, we lost money.

After years of trying, I finally persuaded Gordon Walsh to join us as Interturbine's CEO, and help turn things around. Gordon was a 20 year veteran of General Electric, where he had served as Division CEO.

Just weeks after Gordon's arrival, we faced the biggest crisis in our 40 year history: an Air New Zealand jet engine exploded on the ground. Fortunately, there were no injuries. Six more engine failures followed, causing New Zealand air authorities to ground the entire fleet, and launch an investigation.

The parts with an Interturbine serial number were suspected to be outside of specifications. Air New Zealand sued us for over $40 million, for revenues lost from the grounding of the fleet, as well as the damage to the engines and aircraft, and the cost of leasing replacement aircraft. We soon received similar claims from seven other airlines.

We called an emergency session of the Interturbine board. Larry Clarkson, senior vice president of Boeing at the time, encouraged us to investigate the problem more thoroughly. That probably saved us from disaster.

Results of a study by P&W were inconclusive; our parts were outside of specifications. But another study showed that Air New Zealand had not followed repair procedures properly, and should have used new (not repaired) parts.

We were able to negotiate Air New Zealand's claim down to $1 million, and get

---

[7] Federal Aviation Association, the U.S. regulatory body for the airline industry.

our insurance company to pay. Interturbine offered Air New Zealand a 5% discount on future work, and they continued doing business with us. But, it was a huge blow to our reputation. I was ready to give the flight repair business away.

Fortunately, Gordon had a different perspective on the situation. I'll let him finish the story:

I saw selling the engine repair division as a strategic move. It had never made any real money; some years, a little plus, and some years, a little minus. Competition was tough, especially from OEMs.[8] Our big problem, though, was that all of our work was on old engine models. The jet-engine manufacturers had promised us licenses to service the new engines coming out in the late 1990s, but they hadn't come through.

Our timing was right. OEMs were buying up small overhaul and repair shops as a way to rapidly expand their aftermarket business. GE had just completed a number of small acquisitions, and there was a lot of pressure on the other OEMs to follow. I knew all the players in the industry, and was able to create a mini-auction. Of the five OEMs I approached, four made offers. We sold to P&W, for a good price, in 1997.

We dubbed this second major exit "the Diamond Deal." After the sale, Interturbine's board and managers began to look for opportunities to reinvest the proceeds.

Acquiring a related company was a strategic opportunity - if not necessity - because of a shift in jet engine manufacturers' purchasing behaviours. Historically, they liked to buy from many, specialized suppliers. Increasingly, they wanted to limit the number of suppliers they dealt with, which meant that smaller suppliers were not likely to survive. Interturbine needed more scale.

A banker was hired, for an acquisition search. Eighteen months went by, with no luck. We couldn't find a quality company that we could afford.

---

[8] OEMs (Original Equipment Manufacturers) would sell parts at low cost, to capture the larger and more lucrative aftermarket business (i.e., service and repair of the equipment).

CHAPTER 2

Interturbine's board and managers decided that the smart thing to do was to sell. It made strategic sense, and addressed some real constraints. For one, a major R&D project was proving to be a very expensive failure. For another, there appeared to be no willing or acceptable successor to Bert, from the Twaalfhoven family ranks.

The banker was consulted again, about how to proceed with a sale. The answer was that the pieces were more valuable than the whole. We approached four major industry players that we thought might be interested. We closed a deal for Interturbine's principal entities with Sulzer, who offered us the most attractive valuation and paid in Euros.

The final price for "the Palladium deal," as we called it, was €120 million, worth $102 million at time of sale. Three years later, a favourable change in exchange rates made that $162 million.

Indivers' revenues were a bit of a rollercoaster, but continued to show strong growth during the turbine focus phase. Over the 1986-1996 period (prior to the sale of the flight engine repair business), they grew from $55 million to $120 million. Post-sale revenues of $72 million had climbed to $90 million by 2000, when Indivers made its final exit. (See Exhibit 2-3)

Deciding to sell Interturbine was probably the biggest decision of my career, but I trusted my board, managers, and the next generation of Twaalfhovens. It was time to move on.

EXHIBIT 2-1

Indivers companies by technology segment

Laundry	Tooling	Turbine	Other
Clothes laundry	**Aluminium extrusion**	**Flight engines**	• Fanamation
• Wasserette Belgium	• Aluminium Extruders	• Danvers Seals	• Gilde Ventures
• Wasserette Germany	• MIFA	• Dayton Process	• Inmet
• Wasserette Holland	**Manufacturing**	• Eldim Boston	• Kemco
• Wasserette Switzerland	• Almax France	• Eldim Holland	• North Atlantic Associates Boston
Dry cleaning	• Almax Holland	• Finco (PW4000)	• North Atlantic Associates Holland
• Ribby	• Almax Italy	•Interturbine Airfoil Dallas	• Omnitech
Car wash	• Almax UK	• Interturbine Airfoil Singapore	• QI-Tech
• Autowasserette Belgium	• Blomix	• Interturbine Boston	
• Auto Wasserette Holland	• Innovent	• Interturbine Casings Dallas	
	• Ramix	• Interturbine Fansteel	
	Support for tool manufacturers	• Interturbine Germany	
	• Alectro Germany	• Interturbine Logistics	
	• Alectro Holland	•Interturbine Stators Los Angeles	
	• Alectro Switzerland	• Interturbine U.S.	
	• Alectro UK	• Interturbine Von der Ardenne	
	• Altap	• Paton Coating Holland	
	• BobCad	• Paton Coating Ukraine	
	• Centriforce	• Spartec	
	• Honeycomb Indianapolis	**Stationary engines**	
	• Lauwers Hapert	• Elbar Argentina	
	• Temper Italia	• Elbar Boston	
	• Troika	• Elbar Hickham	
	• Xycarb	• Elbar Holland	
		• Elbar Poland	
		• Elbar Singapore	
		• Elbar Wood	
		• VacHyd Detroit	
		• VacHyd Indianapolis	
		• VacHyd Montreal	
		•VacHyd Toronto	

Source: Company information

EXHIBIT 2-2

Indivers Revenues 1970-1986

(millions of dollars)

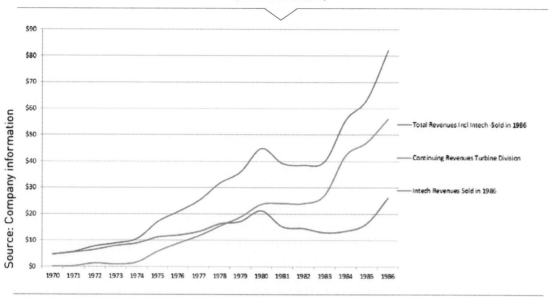

EXHIBIT 2-3

Indivers Revenues 1986-2000

(millions of dollars)

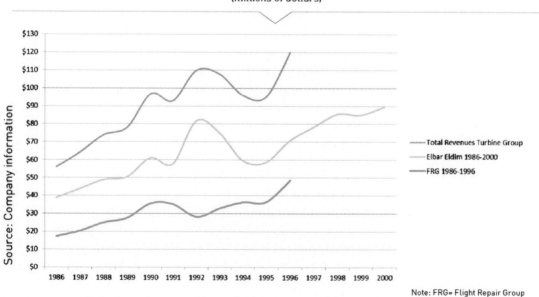

Note: FRG= Flight Repair Group

Aluminium Extruders, Bert's first failure.

Dies for extrusion process, made by Almax, first spin-off and industrial success.

Wasserette, first success. Bert is in back; Elly Koot (former Miss Holland) is in front, standing. (Price: $1 per wash)

Parviz Tavakolly (General Manager of Elbar Holland) explaining the repair of a stationary turbine used in the Middle East.(Price:$ 25 million new/$600.000 repair per turbine)

Celebrating the PW4000 contract in 1984, Dallas
(Bert seated on the right).

Bert announcing contract for Indivers/Eldim
production of F-100 parts, with P&W, 1978
Lomm Holland.

F16 fighter with P&W's F-100 engine.

Pursuing opportunities:
Getting in and getting out

I will never forget my 8 am class with Professor Doriot at HBS. He would always start the same way: "What have you learned that is important, for business?" I developed the habit – one that I still practice – of reading three newspapers before breakfast every day.

My classmate John McDonald also has some vivid memories:

Professor Doriot said: "I want to get you innovating. I want a list each week with 20 ideas for new products and businesses." His point was that entrepreneurship is about idea generation – new products, new markets, new uses and applications for existing products. And, it's not just the first step. Once you've found a good idea, you need to look at opportunities all around it, and then all around them.

Doriot's insistence that we always be on the alert for new opportunities was because you have to look at a lot of them.

I politely listened to one venture capitalist boast about how much money her firm had made, and then asked for the real story. They had reviewed 5,000 proposals, done 1,000 studies to identify 100 opportunities they might want to invest in, and actually invested in 55 of them. Only three were big successes.

Depressing? I don't think so. You just have to follow Doriot's advice!

During my talks, I stress that opportunities are everywhere. You have to look beyond your borders, and deep within your industry to find niches where you can be successful; and then look all around them, for more opportunities. Equally important: you have to know when to get out.

In the following sections, we'll consider the nature of niches, and take a look at how Indivers got in and out of them, to grow into a diversified, multinational enterprise.

The nature of niches

Somewhat ironically, it was by focusing that Indivers was able to diversify. We were always looking for niches, opportunities to solve a customer problem with a new product or service. Art Buckland, a former Indivers CFO, describes it as "sniffing for the open ice; looking for things where other people aren't."

We had lots of curiosity and opportunism at Indivers, but no patented inventions. Tom Liebermann calls that adaptive creation. I'll let him explain:

I heard a talk by a psychologist about a study of political and business leaders, which concluded that all leaders are creative, but fall into two buckets: inventive and adaptive. Gates and Zuckerman and the inventor of the polio vaccine are inventive. Bert and I are adaptive. Laundramat creation is inventive; bringing it to Europe is adaptive. Indivers was 99% adaptive.

It's not just about technology applications, either. You can be adaptive in services, too. For example, I just had my car detailed, which is basically a cleaning service; someone who cleans houses probably had an "aha" moment. I need a haircut. Why not offer a "barbershop in a van" that comes to my home or business every Thursday, for a standing appointment?

We must have looked at thousands of opportunities, over the years. Indivers was interested in niches where we could add value to a product or process, have a competitive advantage, and be a leader in the segment. We looked at entry barriers and other industry characteristics, and considered the resources – human and capital – that would be required to exploit the niche opportunity.

Timing was important, too. We were looking for the proverbial "window of opportunity." During a period of overcapacity in the airline industry, U.S. manufacturers were literally parking extra planes in the desert. We bought their engines cheap, stripped them, and sold the certified parts to our repair customers. That was a temporary situation, but the same principle holds for niches, in general.

Indivers' 65 companies occupied 36 technology niches, primarily in our three major segments (laundry, tooling and turbine). (See Exhibit 3-1 for technology niches) I am sure that we missed many other opportunities along the way, too. That is inevitable, but it still pains me to think about it!

One example. Our Elbar manager proposed starting a service company in Brunei to repair gas turbines on oil platforms, at the suggestion of Shell. We decided against it, feeling that it was too far away to manage properly. In hindsight, a mistake? Our former partner, John Wood, built an impressive niche business doing just that, operating from Scotland.

Technology spinoffs

At Indivers, we often found new opportunities by looking closely at the products or processes we were already working on, and by listening to our customers. Aluminium Extruders offers a good example. That venture, in and of itself, was a failure. But, what we learned from it spawned a series of successful technology spinoffs that ultimately led us to the turbine industry.

Almax was the first spinoff, solving the problem that we ourselves had faced at Aluminium Extruders: the lack of European suppliers able to deliver high-quality dies, fast. From aluminium die-making itself, we moved into support activities.

Heat treating is a critical step in the die-making process, so we initially built Almax factories next to heat treatment service plants. Later, we bought a facility in Italy, for our own and outside customer needs (Temper Italy). We also started a company to manufacture cutting tools used in aluminium extrusion (Altap).

The next opportunity: applying our Almax know-how and approach to non-aluminium processes. We acquired a small tooling company that manufactured plastic injection moulds and dies for the plastic pipe industry (Ramix), and obtained a US license to manufacture plastic blow moulds for tooling plastic bottles for soft drinks and other liquids (Blomix).

The story continues with Almax's adoption of new EDM (electrical/electrochemical discharge machining) technology. We acquired the technology from a manufacturer in Detroit. It was successful at producing high-quality dies at a lower cost and with faster turnaround, using a spark erosion process. What we hadn't considered was the risk of fire from sparks, in a factory built entirely of wood.

I was awakened at 2 am, by my factory manager, shouting outside my bedroom window: "The factory is burning!!" I drove 140 kilometres, arriving at 4 am to find it in ashes. Within five days, we were back in business, in part thanks to the airfreight shipment of two new EDM machines from Detroit to Amsterdam. (Now, that was a confidence booster, I can tell you!)

I went to Detroit, to personally thank the EDM manufacturer. It turned out that EDM also was used for drilling cooling holes in jet-engine fan blades. We hired an engineering student to evaluate the opportunity, and learned that, as part of its purchase of F16 fighter aircraft from Pratt & Whitney, the Dutch government was offering compensation contracts to P&W suppliers.[9] We wanted in on that.

We located a small company in New Jersey with a proprietary hole drilling process, and were able to license its technical know-how. We knew nothing about the industry, so we hired two Rolls Royce executives with jet engine experience to set up a new company called Eldim. We won the F16 contract for hole drilling, our first foray into the turbine industry.

But wait, there's more!

Almax and Eldim were importing graphite for the EDM process from a U.S.-based graphite wholesaler, Electrotools of Chicago. We proposed a partnership, and set up Alectro as a joint venture for Europe. Dr. Gerald Carter, a Cambridge University educated engineer with an MBA from INSEAD, was recruited to run it.

[9] The compensation contract (also known as an offset agreement) was a contract between P&W (through the U.S. government) with the other countries involved in the F16 aircraft project.

Through Alectro, we learned about a company called Xycarb that provided graphite tooling and other specialized services to the semiconductor industry, and formed a joint venture with it as well. Both were very successful.

My final Almax spinoff story involves my oldest son, Bob, and the then new world of CAD/CAM (computer-aided design and manufacturing). As usual, we were eager to exploit a new technology that would improve product cost and quality.

Almax purchased CAD/CAM equipment from Colorado, and set it up in a Holland factory. Bob, a recent MIT engineering graduate, said he could develop the software for half of what the Colorado company was going to charge us ($15,000). Great, we said.

The Dutch government was willing to subsidize part of the investment and development costs, in exchange for allowing others to come in and see the new technology for two hours a day, twice a week. Even better! Bob wrote the software program, and got it to work in our factory.

Bob left Indivers, and formed his own company, adapting the software for use by a variety of tooling companies. BobCad, which began in Germany and now is based in California, has proven very successful. It offers the CAD/CAM software inexpensively, and then makes its money by selling upgrades to a customer base of over 50,000 tool manufacturers.

Industry analysis

I was fortunate, as a student at HBS, to have a course on industry analysis, where we dissected all sorts of businesses. (I find it shocking that such courses are rare, these days.) A deep understanding of an industry allows you to spot – and exploit – opportunities that others will miss.

At Indivers, our systematic study of the jet engine business was a key factor in our success.

When Indivers set up Eldim, we realized that the jet engine industry was a very different world from tooling, which was made up of small, one-man show operations producing specific products for local or regional customers. We were now in a global and much more complicated business, with higher stakes.

We needed to understand the turbine business: the product, the players, and the rules of the game. Step one: find an expert. We recruited Jaap Blaak from the Dutch steel company Hoogovens, to lead Eldim.

To understand the product, we acquired a thousand reverse-engineered drawings of a jet engine. We learned that it had over 25,000 parts, of which 1,000 were specialty products.

We mapped out the jet engine supply chain, and saw that the turbine industry was similar to the auto industry in Japan, with a cascade of specialty product suppliers and a whole chain of processes. From one segment at the third or fourth echelon, you could see spin-off opportunities everywhere.

Designing and building a new engine, we learned, could cost $3 billion. Engine manufacturers usually involved a consortium of industry partners, who would share the considerable risk and costs, in exchange for exclusive manufacturing and/or service contracts.

Finally, we found that component suppliers had to be certified not by the airline – your customer – but by the engine manufacturers (Rolls Royce, Pratt & Whitney, General Electric, etc.).

Our conclusion: there were some tough entry barriers but, once you were in, it was beautiful. (I joke that it was like my father's business. As a doctor, he made most of his money not from delivering babies but from the lifelong "maintenance" work.)

The rest, as they say, is history. Turbine components became Indivers' growth engine. (See Chapter 2, for more details)

Figure 3-1 P&W jet engine component drawing
Product 60 year life cycle-25.000 parts

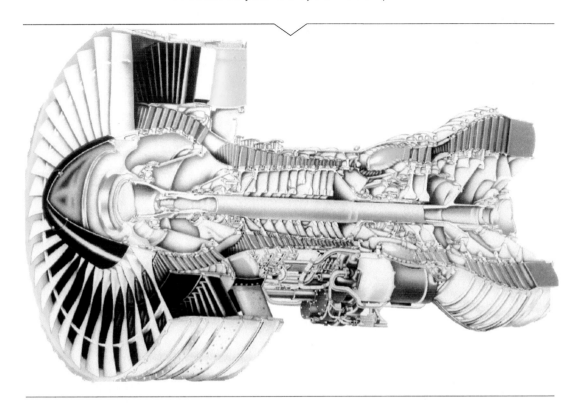

Going beyond your borders

Transferring ideas from one part of the world to another was a mainstay of Indivers' success. It worked both ways. Most of the opportunities we pursued in our early years came from North America. In turn, many of our successes involved transferring what we had learned (or developed) to emerging markets.

VacHyd Singapore is a good example of both: acquiring a new technology from the U.S. and, then, exporting it to Asia. Here's how that unfolded.

Indivers had some extra cash in the early 1970s, and decided to increase our presence in the U.S. by making a small acquisition. After some searching, we found a company called VacHyd that did heat treating for turbine manufacturers in several U.S. cities, and had a joint venture in Germany, to service Lufthansa. We bought it.

We also were interested in expanding into Asian markets.

In 1975, the Singapore government was advised by Dr. Winsemius, its UN Economic Advisor, to promote the development of its aerospace infrastructure. Dr. Winsemius was from Holland, and I made a point of contacting him to understand Singapore's agenda. Next, a call on a fellow HBS alumnus, who was in charge of the Singapore government's Economic Development Board (EDB).

The EDB agreed to be co-shareholder of a new VacHyd subsidiary in Singapore. We shipped over a vacuum furnace from our German factory, and began offered heat treating services to the Far East, including Australian Airlines and Singapore Airlines. The venture was very successful, and we later bought back the EDB's shares.

It was my plan from the beginning to build a multinational enterprise. I developed that perspective at HBS, interacting with classmates with experience in many industries, around the world. Over our 40 year history, Indivers had operations in 14 countries, serving several hundred customers in over 40 countries. (See Exhibit 3-2)

Venturing beyond national boundaries has been a challenge for European business.[10] In today's global economy, information flows fast and freely, and markets are interconnected. The dynamics may have changed (e.g., emerging countries look to Europe for ideas; India and China are entrepreneurial hotbeds) but the multinational imperative remains the same for dynamic entrepreneurs.

Getting out

There are two kinds of exits, as I see it: voluntary and forced. The latter, which I call failures, are described in some detail in Chapter 4, where the chapter title

---

[10] David Birch's work showed that American gazelles expanded across the entire U.S. and to international markets, while European gazelles tended to remain at home.

sums it up: "Taking risks: Failing forward." Some failures are inevitable. The good news is that failures accounted for just 16 of Indivers' 40 exits, over the years.

Indivers never entered a niche with the intent of exiting, but we were prepared to do so – voluntarily -when it made good business sense. Knowing when to exit is as much of an art as a science, and requires some discipline; it's easy to hang on too long. Some of our exits were strategic, and sometimes we simply needed the money.

Products, markets, players - competitors, suppliers, and customers – and the environment (e.g., exchange rates, regulations) can and will change. You need to be aware of the changes, and understand the implications for your business. Sometimes, the changes make an attractive business less so, and sometimes they open up possibilities for new and different ventures.

"When the boundaries surrounding a niche disappear, it's no longer a niche." (A colleague made that astute comment.) Being the first on the scene with a unique solution to a customer problem is a winning formula, but competition inevitably appears, and you lose your advantage. Time to look elsewhere, for new technologies and markets, but that requires both time and money.

Trade-offs have to be made.

Indivers' major exits offer good examples of strategic moves, either to exit a business segment that no longer appeared viable (e.g., flight repair), or reallocate resources to a better opportunity (i.e., from peripheral graphite businesses to core turbine activities). Both of those large sales were to major aviation industry players.

The majority of our exits, however, were individual, small company sales. In some cases, a current Indivers manager would be eager for the opportunity to become an entrepreneur, and buy the business. (We encouraged that, even helping with the financing, at times.) In other cases, the business was a joint venture, and our partner would buy us out.

Any regrets? Yes. Sometimes we exited early, because we needed the cash, and

CHAPTER 3

the venture proved to be a big winner.

Aalberts Industries is a good example of a missed opportunity. Indivers co-financed the industrial start-up, and sold our 30% of shares a year later, for less than half a million Euros. Last week, the company announced revenues of over €2 billion. Another example: Gilde Venture, where I sold my 25% of the founding shares. Today, it's a billion dollar venture capital firm.

Timing is crucial, whether you're getting in or getting out.

EXHIBIT 3-1

Indivers' technology niches

Laundry	Tooling	Turbine	Other
• Automatic washers	**Aluminium extrusion**	**Flight engines**	• Inspection robotics
• Automatic driers	• Aluminium extru-	• Manufacturing of	• Market research
• Dry cleaning	sion for ladders and	honeycomb cones	• Venture capital
• Car wash	windows	• Repair of:	
	Manufacturing	- Bearing houses	
	• Dies for aluminium	- Casings	
	extrusion	- Stators	
	• Moulds for plastics	• Manufacturing and	
	pipes	repair of:	
	• Moulds for plastic	- Blades/vanes	
	bottles	- Seals	
	• Dies for computer chip	• Processes:	
	manufacturing	- Ceramic coating	
	• Graphite dies for	- Heat treatment	
	semi-conductor	- Hole drilling	
	* Honeycomb vacuum	**Stationary engines**	
	moulds for diapers	• Manufacturing of	
	Support for tool manu-	combusters	
	facturers	• Repair of casings	
	• CAD/CAM systems	• Manufacturing and	
	• Conical tools	repair of blades/	
	• Graphite	vanes	
	• Heat treatment	• Overhaul of marine	
		turbines	
		• Processes:	
		- Brazing	
		- Coating	
		- Heat treatment	
		- Welding	

Source: Company information

EXHIBIT 3-2

Indivers' multinational operations

Holland	Europe	Americas	Asia
Holland	**Belgium**	**Argentina**	**China**
• Alectro Holland	• Autowasserette Belgium	• Elbar Argentina	• QI-Tech
• Almax Holland	• Ribby	**Canada**	**Singapore**
• Altap	• Wasserettte Belgium	• VacHyd Montreal	• Interturbine Airfoil
• Aluminium	**France**	• VacHyd Toronto	Singapore
Extruders	• Almax France	**U.S.**	• Elbar Singapore
• Autowasserette	**Germany**	• Bobcad	
Holland	• Alectro Germany	• Danvers Seals	
• Blomix	• Interturbine Germany	* Dayton Boston	
• Centriforce	• Interturbine	• Elbar Boston	
• Elbar Holland	Logistics	• Elbar Hickham	
• Eldim Holland	• Interturbine Von der	• Eldim Boston	
• Finco/PW4000	Ardenne	• Fanamation	
• Gilde Ventures	• Troika	• Honeycomb	
• Interturbine Fansteel	• Wasserette Germany	Indianapolis	
• Louwers Hapert	**Italy**	• InMet	
• MIFA	• Almax Italy	• Innovent	
• North Atlantic	• Temper Italia	• Interturbine Airfoil	
Assiocates Holland	**Poland**	Dallas	
• Paton Coating	• Elbar Poland	• Interturbine Boston	
Holland	**Switzerland**	• Interturbine Caslings	
• Ramix	• Alectro Switzerland	Dallas	
• Wasserette Holland	• Wasserette Switzerland	• Interturbine Stators	
• Xycarb	**Ukraine**	Los Angeles	
	• Paton Coating Ukraine	• Interturbine U.S.	
	United Kingdom	• North Atlantic	
	• Almax UK	Associates Boston	
	• Alectro UK	• Omnitech	
	• Elbar Wood (Scotland)	• Omnitech	
	• Kemco	• VacHyd Detroit	
	• Spartec	• VacHyd Indianapolis	

Technology spin -offs

ALUMINIUM EXTRUSIONS

PLASTIC BOTTLES AND PIPES

BOB-CAD U.S.A

CENTRIFORCE EUROPE

TOOLS- DIES FOR ALUMINIUM

ALTAP CUTTING TOOL

SPARK: EDMECMLASER

Tool diversification, from aluminium extrusion, to dies and beyond.

Almax fire, caused by spark erosion

Almax, back in full production, 5 days after the fire

A complex of 7 specialized Indivers plants in Holland

VacHyd's Singapore plant

Celebrating Interturbine's joint venture with Paton in Kiev, Ukraine.

Indivers board members at the VacHyd Los Angeles plant,

Technology spin-offs

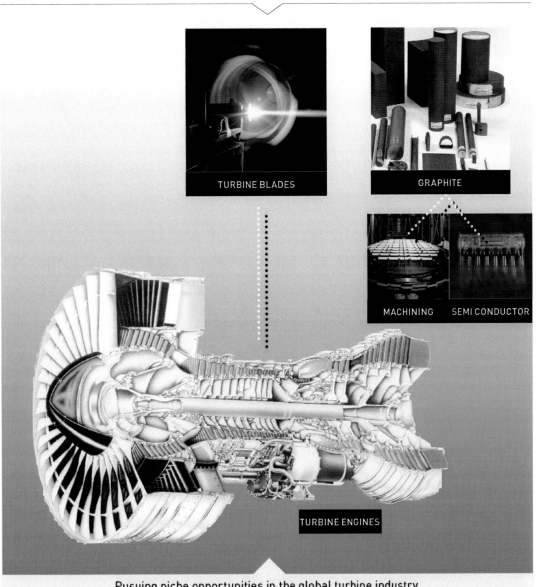

TURBINE BLADES

GRAPHITE

MACHINING   SEMI CONDUCTOR

TURBINE ENGINES

Pusuing niche opportunities in the global turbine industry.

Technology spin-offs

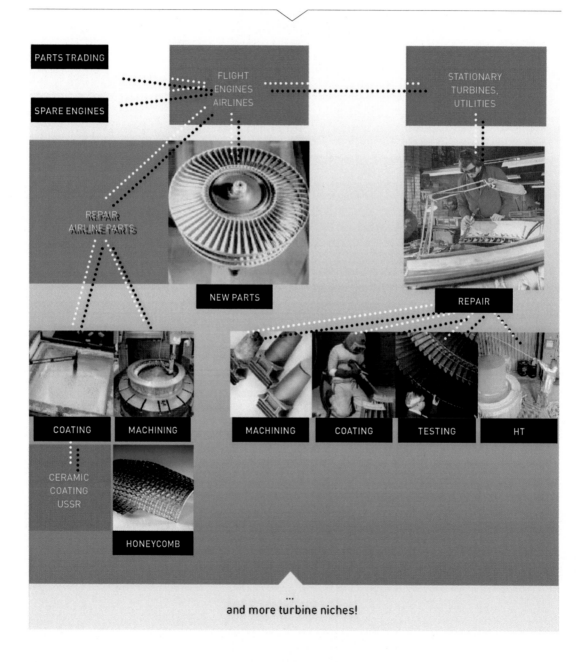

PARTS TRADING

SPARE ENGINES

FLIGHT ENGINES AIRLINES

STATIONARY TURBINES, UTILITIES

REPAIR AIRLINE PARTS

NEW PARTS

REPAIR

COATING

MACHINING

MACHINING

COATING

TESTING

HT

CERAMIC COATING USSR

HONEYCOMB

...
and more turbine niches!

Talking Risks:
Failing forward

"Why do you talk about your failures so much, Bert?"

I often answer that question by quoting a Chinese proverb:

失败是成功之母.

"Failure is the mother of success."

Entrepreneurship is about doing things that are new and different, which inevitably will involve some risk, and some failures. Thomas Edison said: "I have not failed. I've just found 10,000 ways that won't work." Sometimes, a "failure" is just part of the process.

In the spirit of learning from failure, let's take a look at Indivers' experience. I'll start with an overview and some examples of failures, and end with some thoughts about "failing forward."

Indivers' failures

Business failure can be defined a number of ways: going bankrupt, falling short of financial or other business targets, or not meeting your personal goals for the venture.

For me, entrepreneurship is about identifying opportunities and turning them into realities, so I define failure as walking away from the opportunity, involuntarily. Of the 65 companies we started at Indivers, we had to walk away from sixteen, for a total loss of €52 million+ over 40 years. (See Exhibit 4-1)

Indivers' failures are not concentrated in a particular product category or geography. They are not limited to any particular time period, either. The first one occurred in 1959, and the last in 2001. What is notable though, is the size of the failures, over time. Steve Ricci explains it well:

An entrepreneur's risk tolerance changes over time. In the early days, you have nothing to lose, so you place bets that may be small in absolute terms, but big for you at the time. Down the road, you have built value, but don't have the balance sheet to withstand a shock, so you become risk averse. Later, you have more resources, and can withstand the storm.

Some of my failures, ironically, stemmed from the enthusiasm that also made me a good entrepreneur: eagerness to seize opportunities. Indivers sometimes probably was trying to do too much, too quickly. That can result in spreading your resources too thin, expanding without the right local management in place, or not doing a thorough enough check on the technology or market potential.

Live and learn.

Risks manifest themselves in lots of different ways, and sometimes seem to come out of nowhere. Indivers' failures generally can be traced to some common underlying causes - market, technology, finance, culture, operations, and management – often in combination. (Again, see Exhibit 4-1) Each failure has its own unique story, of course.

In Chapter 5, we will look at one of our largest failures, the PW4000 project. Here are four more illustrative case studies from Indivers' experience: Aluminium Extruders, QI -Tech, Interturbine Paton, and North Atlantic Associates.

Aluminium Extruders Holland: Squeezed out

One of my projects at Alcan was to assess a proposal to partner with a professor in Vancouver on an aluminium extrusion business start-up.

The extrusion process, I learned, is like squeezing a tube of toothpaste. You start with the end product in mind (e.g., a ladder). Based on product specifications, a die with a shaped opening is created. During extrusion, a billet (the aluminium) is softened by heat, and then forced through the die by a powerful hydraulic device. Extruded material emerges as an elongated piece with the same profile as the die opening. The extrusion is cooled, stretched, sawed to the desired length, and heat treated in ovens.

Our market research revealed that aluminium consumption was low in Europe, because aluminium windows and ladders were not yet being produced there. Future prospects looked good, though, with a building boom underway. And, competition was still light; there were only five or six aluminium extruders in operation.

I had an idea: transfer aluminium extrusion technology and expertise from North America to Holland. (It turned out that a Dutch friend at Alcan had been thinking the same thing.)

When Maria received an inheritance from her father, I was in a position to pursue the opportunity. I left Alcan. At Professor Doriot's suggestion, I took a posi tion at Ladenberg Thalmann, a boutique investment bank on Wall Street. (He had pointed out my lack of experience with start-ups.) I analysed business plans from would-be entrepreneurs, while beginning my own search for a business partner.

At the suggestion of a colleague, I contacted Kruger Metals in Montreal. In 1960, we decided to form a joint venture: Aluminium Extrusions Holland. Kruger would provide a second hand hydraulic press and technical support, in exchange for a 60% share of equity. I would put up $100,000 cash, for a 40% share, and serve as CEO.

Meanwhile, I had made a trip to Holland, to talk with the Dutch government about subsidies that I knew were available for new businesses. They agreed to finance the land and buildings for a factory. A meeting with a window manu- facturer yielded a two year contract. Factory construction began. Things were looking good!

Maria and I moved the family to Holland, with great excitement.

Kruger shipped the equipment from Canada, and sent two technicians to install it. We immediately ran into press problems; the machines weren't extruding to specification. Eventually, we realized that the Canadian installers had not factored in European electrical differences. It took almost a year to resolve the problem.

Orders were cancelled, and we went from a two year order position to one month.

We faced another problem, too: production delays stemming from having to import dies from Boston and Chicago. (There were no suppliers in Europe.) Because dies represented just 3-4% of product costs, architects liked to customize, a lot. A large order, for us, was a five-day production run; and we needed 20 new dies a week, not once a month as originally thought.

We lost all of our equity in two years. Kruger fired me, and brought in its own team. After three years, it sold the company (including my shares) to Reynolds Metals USA. I filed a lawsuit, which Alcan paid for, because they wanted to keep Reynolds out of Europe. I finally recouped my investment, two years later.

On the positive side, that failure led to a better opportunity for Indivers: die-making for European extruders! And, the epilogue for Aluminum Extruders? It is now owned by Alcoa, and was only recently downsized, after three decades of expansion.

QI-Tech, China: Double jeopardy

This story involves a failed effort to save a failing high-tech company. It starts in California, and ends in China.

My oldest son, Mark,[11] and two Stanford University classmates invented new technology for coordinate measurement machines (CMMs), which are used as inspec-

---

[11] Mark held MBA and engineering degrees from Stanford.

tion robots in the car, airline and defence industries. Their innovations: a linear motor allowed the robot to move more quickly; and installation of the robot on air balloons reduced vibrations, and kept it accurate even during earthquakes. They experimented with the technology at Indivers' factories in Los Angeles.

In 1985, the inventors founded a company called Fanamation, and named Mark president. Indivers invested $30,000, for a minority position. Fanamation was able to raise an additional $8 million of seed capital from angel investors, and five venture capital firms.

Fanamation caught the attention of the inspection industry, and attracted several large customers for its $150,000 machines. The U.S. defence industry became a major client. The Chinese Ministry of Aviation, another large client, expressed interest in a partnership in 1991, but Fanamation decided against it. By 1992, Fanamation's revenues had reached $6 million, and demand was still growing.

Mark saw an opportunity to become a global player in CMM, which was dominated by Brown & Sharp (Rhode Island) and Zeiss/Leitz (Germany). More funding would be required. He had almost lined up the financing, when stock markets around the world crashed, in 1987. The funding dried up, and he turned to Indivers for help.

In 1992, Indivers invested $2 million in Fanamation, for a controlling interest. We also acquired a 50% interest in Kemco Derby, a UK-based manufacturer of low-end robots. The following year, Fanamation and Kemco were combined into a new entity called InMet, which promptly bought a share of OmniTech, a Chicago-based CMM service company.

Then, the problems began.

A huge order from Chrysler Canada was good news, but it meant refusing other orders for six months; Fanamation factory capacity was maxed out. Then, a recession hit, and the Pentagon slashed its spending. By 1994, InMet had lost $8 million, and was almost bankrupt. Indivers decided to stop further support.

The Chinese Ministry of Aviation, which owned an inspection robot manufacturing company called QQMF in Tsingtao, remained interested. QQMF had a monopoly on the Chinese market for CCM, and also owned automobile companies. Its Chief Technology Officer had identified Fanamation and InMet as being leading-edge, and was keen to obtain their know-how.

In 1994, a 50/50 deal was struck to form Qinshao Indivers Technology, or QI-Tech. QQMF brought facilities, 130 technical personnel, and China market access. Fanamation/InMet brought patents, know-how, machinery and equipment, several engineers, and knowledge of the Western market.

Mark became CEO, and moved his family to Tsingtao. Fanamation's manufacturing equipment was shipped to China. A dozen Chinese engineers were trained at Indivers' Singapore plant. The Chinese Technical Officer was trained at the University of Eindhoven, in Holland.

As CEO, Mark faced many challenges, and would have to make significant and difficult changes.

Language and cultural differences were major barriers. Communications were problematic. Business practices needed to be altered. (For example, the Chinese booked their orders and profits, before production of the order even began.) Productivity was poor and work force reduction required, which ran counter to Chinese Communist rules.

On the brighter side, Mark became recognized as one of China's first high-tech business people. When German Prime Minister Helmut Kohl visited Tsingtao, a former German colony, Mark was introduced to him as a leading foreign entrepreneur, receiving worldwide press coverage.

However, QI-Tech continued to lose money.

Mark and the chairman of the board (yes, that would be Bert) parted. Mark attended the Advanced Management Program at HBS, and became CEO of the Asian Division of a large U.S. company. Today, he is an entrepreneur in Shanghai. (And, father and son have reconciled.)

Indivers decided to end our investment in QI-Tech, where we had lost several million dollars over the 1995-1998 period. We were unwilling to fund expansion plans, especially given that the business did not fit with our core turbine strategy. We also were struggling with the financial implications of the Air New Zealand crisis.

In the fall of 1998, we sent our Indivers business development manager to China, to negotiate a sale. Brown & Sharp, which saw QI-Tech as an entry point to the Chinese market, was interested. We sold our shares to them that year. Some years later, QI-Tech and Brown & Sharp were acquired by a Swedish company called Hexagon.

Today, QI-Tech has over $300 million in revenues. I wish that we had kept some shares!

Interturbine Paton: Betting on the future

We knew that General Electric, Pratt & Whitney, and Rolls Royce were developing next-generation jet engines that operated at very high temperatures. We saw an opportunity: a specialty thermal barrier coating for engine components.

We learned that the Russian military had mastered the technology for its MIG fighters, using a ceramic coating process developed by the Paton Institute of Kiev, Ukraine. We were all charged up, and made contact with Professor Paton.

In December 1993, we formed a joint venture with the Paton Institute, for their expertise and use of their R&D facilities. In June 1994, we established a second team in Holland, shipping machines from the Ukraine. Interturbine Paton was set up as a new company.

It became apparent that the Russians had much lower quality standards than our commercial customers; 80% of the MIG engine coating that was produced had to be scrapped. The 20% that was usable only lasted 1,000 hours; our customers expected 20,000. We concluded that the equipment was to blame.

With financial support from the German Research Office and the Dutch Aerospace Lab, Indivers formed a 50/50 joint venture with a high-temperature furnace builder (Von Der Ardenne) in Dresden. They produced a new machine for ceramic coating.

Two years later, in 1999, we were finally operational, at ten times our original estimate for the project. But the quality problems persisted. We consulted with a Penn State University expert in the field, and a retired executive from a competitor. They told us that our coating methodology was wrong.

By 2000, we thought we had fixed the problem. We hired a Swiss expert as manager, and won a development contract from GE for its new JSF (Joint Strike Fighter) plane, being developed for the U.S. Defence Department.

It had been expensive, however, to master the technology. Also, other suppliers had come on stream, with U.S. operations. For U.S. components manufacturers, it did not make economic sense to ship parts to Holland to be coated. Our cumulative losses came to €18 million (€6 million, offset by the GE order).

Interturbine's 2001 sale to Sulzer included Paton (with the GE contract). That allowed us to recover our money from the Paton failure, but the Dutch government lost millions on its investment.

North Atlantic Associates: Out of control

Every summer, Indivers hired university students to conduct competitive analysis. In the fall of 1980, a recent HBS graduate who had worked with us one summer came to me with an idea: why not commercialize those activities, targeting them to the need and resources of SMEs?

I had a quick study done on the economics of management consulting firms, and decided to partner with him. North Atlantic Associates (NAA) was founded in March 1981, with $100,000 capital.

NAA would provide high-quality services, priced below what big firms like McKinsey charged, using a traditional pyramid structure.[12] To save money, we would co-locate offices with Indivers in Amsterdam, and with one of our subsidiaries in Boston. In December, we began assembling a team, and prospecting for clients (initially within Indivers).

We assembled a 22-person team. Management included my HBS business partner, an ex-McKinsey consulting partner, and Indivers' former SVP of business development. They recruited eight Harvard MBA students, who were joined by an INSEAD student towards the end of the summer. They also hired five university students for research support, and five staff (for graphics and administrative support).

Five projects were sold, for the summer, to Indivers subsidiaries. Each project had a dedicated team, and a work plan that extended over 12-14 weeks, and included three phases: industry overview and initial problem diagnosis; detailed market and competitive analysis; and strategy and recommendations. Each phase concluded with a client presentation and discussion.

Problems surfaced almost immediately. NAA lost $100,000 in just six months. Projects were not completed before the end of summer, and a portfolio of new work was not developed. We liquidated the company in January 1982, and wrote off the investment.

What went wrong, we wondered? Here are the results of a post-mortem analysis:

- Senior management was unable to work together effectively, leading to the early departure of one partner.
- Initial success selling projects built unrealistic expectations about the size of the market, and how long it takes to land new clients.

---

[12] Large consulting firms typically used senior MBAs as project heads and business developers plus a larger pool of university graduates for research and analysis, to leverage experience, increase capacity, and lower costs.

- Inexperienced team members and lack of proper project planning and management resulted in time and cost overruns; profitability and cash flow suffered.
- Constant fire fighting distracted management from focusing on business development to generate a pipeline of projects for the fall.
- NAA was unable to meet payroll and pay its bills; staff and vendor confidence flagged.

The epilogue: my founding partner restarted the business, experienced another failure, and eventually was successful.

Failing forward

I see failure as a stepping stone, not a stumbling block. It is common wisdom that we learn more from our failures than our successes. You can not only survive, but learn from business setbacks, all the better to anticipate and manage future challenges. And, sometimes a failure will open up a new opportunity.

Certainly, I don't like to walk away from a business. If something isn't working, I will look for another way. But, as my friend Howard Stevenson puts it: "You have to be realistic about the dead, the living dead, and the successes – and be good at not sticking with the first two."

Indivers ultimately was a success despite – sometimes, because of - our failures along the way. It's about luck and tenacity.

EXHIBIT 4-1

Indivers' failures

Year	Company and location	Business	Size of loss	Cause of failure
1959	Auto Wasserette, CH	Car wash	€136,000	*Technology and market* – Water pressure damaged lacquer of cars popular in Switzerland
1960	Aluminium Extruders, NL	Aluminium extrusion	€340,000	*Technology, market and finance* – Delays adapting U.S.-sourced technology, loss of customers, competition, and withdrawal of majority owner
1968	Almax, France	Tooling – Aluminium extrusion	€294,000	*Operations and culture* – Paris workers unwilling to commute to relocated plant
1979	Troika, Germany	Tooling - CAD/CAM system	€45,000	*Technology and market* – U.S.-sourced system did not meet stricter German quality standards
1981	North Atlantic Associates	Management consulting	€128,000	*Management* – Inadequate planning/business development, project management, and controls
1982	Elbar, Singapore	Turbine – Stationary repair	€170,000	*Management and culture* – Inadequate resources (needed local talent)
1985	Elbar, Boston	Turbine – Stationary repair	€85,000	*Management and market* – Inadequate resources and unanticipated competition
1985	Interturbine, Dallas	Turbine – Flight repair	€966,000	*Management* – Fraud (false reporting of work activity and revenues)
1986	Danvers Seals, Boston	Turbine - Flight repair	€85,000	*Market* - Unanticipated competition
1986	Elbar, Holland	Turbine – Stationary repair	€320,000	*Technology* – Requirements were beyond our capabilities
1988	QI-Tech, China	Inspection robotics	€5.5 million	*Culture, management and operations* - Unfamiliar business practices, work force challenges, and quality problems
1990	PW4000 (Finco), NL	Turbine – Flight components	€13.6 million	*Technology, market, finance* –Technology development project delays, customer acceptance costs, and withdrawal of bank partners
1990	Waterwall, Elbar, NL	Turbine – Stationary repair	€908,000	*Technology* – Massive furnace for heat treatment failed to scale up properly
1994	Interturbine, Air New Zealand	Turbine – Flight repair	€1.7 million	*Technology* – Inadequate quality control
1996	Interturbine, Holland and Germany	Turbine – Flight repair	€8 million	*Market and finance* - Lack of unique market made them unattractive to P&W (purchaser of other flight repair operations)
2000	Paton, Ukraine and NL	Turbine – Flight component	€18.1 million	*Technology and market* - Technology development delays, and unanticipated competition

Source: Company information

71

Marshalling resources:
The power of networking

"If you know what you don't know, you're a winner."

That's one of my favourite slogans. There's an important caveat, though: you'd better know someone who does know! I knew nothing about jet engines, but that didn't stop me from getting into the business. What it did mean was that I spent a lot of time finding technical expertise.

"When in Rome, do as the Romans do."

Another favourite slogan! How could a small Dutch company expand into Italy, the U.S., China, and Russia? The answer was networking: hire a local manager, get a local banker, make sure someone on your boards knows the region, and reach out to local government officials.

> *The single most important role of the entrepreneur is to evangelize and recruit other people to share his vision. Bert credits a lot of his success to his network, but it is in the context of sharing his vision, and his enthusiasm. He was able to attract top talent. He would work and work to make an opportunity it happen, romancing it – for example, looking for financial partners - until it was affordable or sufficiently rewarding that it would pay for itself.*
>
> *– Steve Ricci*

To me, it comes down to this: you can't do it alone.

In this chapter, we'll talk briefly about how to build and use networks. Then, we'll look at the breadth and depth of Indivers' networks, and how we used them to spot opportunities, marshal resources, and put plans in place to execute our business ideas.

Networking and the entrepreneur

Networking comes naturally to some people, but it's also a skill that can be learned.

I learned about networking at HBS, and HBS is still my most important network. Its alumni, students, faculty and administrators are an incredible a source of talent, advice, and introductions to high-level contacts in business and government across the globe. When traveling, I always check to see if there are any alumni in the city being visited, and give them a call. (I am happy to reciprocate.)

I spend a lot of time building and nurturing networks, often face-to-face. It helps to genuinely enjoy talking to people! I'm always taking names: Who is good at this? Who is interested in that? It's about collecting resources.

Bert and I were at an industry convention in New York. I told him that I had met with global upply manager of a major customer. He said: "Get me a meeting with the President." I did, and they had a nice talk about entrepreneurship, family, anything but business.

- Gordon Walsh

We'd be in the car, going to a meeting. Bert would be reading the newspaper, and suddenly say: "Look at this! We have to get hold of this guy!" There was massive value to meeting people, to him, for bouncing ideas around, andgetting market intelligence.

- Nadia Hill Spendal

Networking also can involve building communities of people with shared interests. At Indivers, for many years, we hosted an annual "mini Davos"[13] either at Indivers' offices or at my family's Swiss ski chalet, inviting our board plus business and academic leaders from Europe and the U.S. to talk about economic and business issues. In my EFER work, creating networks among academics, entrepreneurs, and supporters of entrepreneurship has been a major thrust.

Every professional and social interaction is an opportunity to make a connection that could be useful in the future. For an entrepreneur trying to break into a new field, networking also is a way to open doors, by elevating the visibility of your business. (Many people thought Indivers was much larger than we really were.)

Finally, because entrepreneurs are constantly facing a shortage of resources, you have to be creative. You get good at using other people's resources, because often you can't afford (or don't want) to own or employ them yourself. Networking is a way to access ideas, information, talent, financing, good will, and whatever else you may need.

Indivers' networks

One of the objectives of the University of Cambridge study described in Chapter 2 was to examine the processes that entrepreneurs use to create and build ventures. The researchers quickly observed the importance of Indivers' networks,[14] depicting them as shown in Figure 5-1.

---

[13] Davos, Switzerland is the site of the World Economic Forum
[14] Source: "Indivers Research Project," Y. Myint, Centre for Entrepreneurial Learning, Judge Business School, University of Cambridge, 2006.

CHAPTER 5

Figure 5-1 Indivers Networks

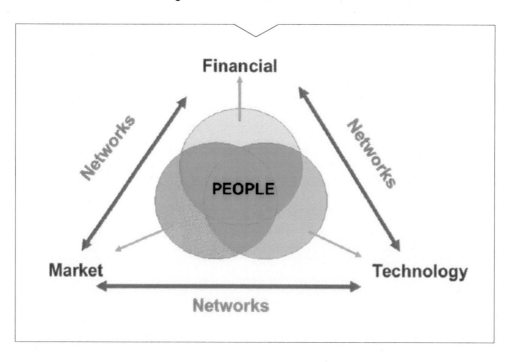

As a high-tech, global, growth-oriented company, Indivers did indeed need technology, market, and financial resources. (I would add that we also needed management expertise, especially as we got bigger.) Our networks were the way to do it, and a big part of my role – as the founder and owner – was to build them, first with individuals and then entire organizations.

I define my network broadly, including other entrepreneurs, managers (and alumni) of my company, board members, people in large organizations who could provide resources or help forge strategic alliances, links with universities and research institutions, and local connections around the world. Even with institutions, the personal connection was essential.

On the following pages, we'll look at some of the Indivers networks identified by the University of Cambridge researchers.

Research network

At Indivers, we were always on the lookout for leading edge technologies, in or around our niche markets.

Whenever we discovered a research centre doing leading edge work (often through a board member or manager), I would find out who I knew there, identify the key academic person, and try to set up a meeting. For the researchers, Indivers offered a window to the real world, an opportunity to learn about the industry and applications of their technology.

We developed relationships with a total of 25 organizations in ten countries over the years, including departments of major universities and independent research institutes. (See Exhibit 5-1). Each was highly specialized. For example, Penn State University had a huge ceramics department, Leuven was strong in laser drillings, and Eindhoven knew all about inspection robotics.

In a few cases, we had formal contracts for R&D projects, but most were informal relationships. If we had a technical question, we knew who to call for advice. I would attend each research centre's annual meeting, taking two Indivers managers with me. It was a chance for us to network not just with research staff, but all the people associated with the institution and its work.

University network

Each year, Indivers hired a crop of summer students. We took a few undergraduate engineering students, but mainly we were looking for MBAs with technical undergraduate degrees and/or work experience with someone in the turbine industry, such as Rolls Royce. By going to universities around the world, we also were able to tap into talent with local experience and contacts.

We had two objectives for our summer program. First, we strongly believed in competitive analysis but couldn't afford to build an in-house group, so students' research skills were invaluable. Second, it was a potential source of new managerial talent for the company. Each year, we would offer permanent positions to a number of students, after they graduated.

Students sometimes would contact Indivers about a summer job, after I gave a talk at their universities. (I did that quite frequently.) But, I also methodically reviewed resumes, and targeted top prospects for personal follow up, each year. As one of my colleagues puts it: "There is no substitute for CEO story telling."

In total, Indivers employed 650 summer students from 21 institutions in 10 countries, over our forty years. (See Exhibit 5-2)

Indivers managers and board

As Indivers grew and expanded into new areas, we drew in people with the knowledge, skills, experience and contacts that we needed to run the business. Exhibit 5-3 shows some of our 30+ managers, from more than 10 different countries. Over time, they included engineers and MBAs, as well as industry veterans. (See Chapter 6, for more about Indivers' people and culture.)

We also were able to assemble outside boards that provided valuable advice, access to talent, and connections with major customers and other industry players. Indivers' board of directors usually had five or six members at a time, drawn from virtually all parts of our ecosystem. (See Exhibit 5-4) Its members included industry and academic leaders, financial partners, and government institutions, of many nationalities. (Of note: In Holland, the company chairman is not allowed to sit on

---

The boards of most start-ups typically include family members and an accountant. An outside board wasn't necessary for Indivers, as a private company, but Bert valued it highly. He had an ability to bring together important people who just enjoyed working with him; it wasn't about prestige.

- Felix Twaalfhoven

the board.)

Our board was very engaged in the business. Board members would get frequent reports from Indivers managers and myself. Four times a year, we would meet somewhere in the world, at an Indivers location. Our board provided input to planning and other routine business matters, and saved us during more than one crisis (e.g., the Air New Zealand affair).

Financial partners

There is a saying, among entrepreneurs, that your first investors are "family, friends, and fools." I benefited from the first, through my father-in-law's bequest.

Finding risk capital is an on-going challenge, for a growth company like Indivers. Financing a venture often involved more than one source, and more than one type of support. Indivers was very creative at rallying financing, thanks to our very able CFO, Aad van Noord.

We developed some criteria for when and how to establish financial partnerships.

First, we insisted on a long term horizon. Potential investors often were looking for great results in just two or three years, especially for start-up ventures. We knew from experience that it would take at least five years. Second, we were looking for more than money. We expected our partners to bring industry, country, and customer knowledge and relationships, too.

As Indivers grew and built a track record, it became easier to attract investors. But explaining the nature of an opportunity to people unfamiliar with your industry can be challenging, especially for new and complex technologies and niches.

During a presentation to 300 bankers in Luxembourg, I showed a large picture of a jet engine, and asked if anyone knew what it was. Only two hands went up, both from former Rolls Royce managers. The bank that they represented bought 10% of Interturbine's shares, and stayed with us for 20 years. It was worth the wait. They put in $400,000, and Indivers bought them out for $12 million.

Over the years, Indivers built a highly interconnected network of 17 major supporters in Europe, the U.S. and Asia. They included government agencies, venture capital firms, and major banks. (See Exhibit 5-5) We also established local banking relationships in 13 different countries.

Government subsidies were an important funding mechanism for Indivers, all over the world. (They remain an important and often overlooked resource for today's entrepreneurs, too.) The Marshall Plan, which was established after WWII by the U.S. to help rebuild Europe, was a source of venture capital in our early years. European institutions took over the role, after the program ended.

Knowing what subsidies were being offered, and how to position Indivers for them required networking; I had many government contacts. We learned about and were awarded R&D subsidies from Aerospace Institutes in Holland and Germany, which put us in the thick of the industry. We kept them highly informed about the business, with regular reports and meetings.

Another example: When the Dutch government bought F16 planes from America, part of the deal was that a certain amount of after-market support would be done as an offset agreement in the European countries involved in the partnership. We learned about that, muzzled our way to the table, and got a piece. We also were able to get research grants from a big European initiative for commercial research, for the project.

Large banks were an early and on-going source of capital for Indivers, around the world. For example, the Development Bank of Singapore (DBS) enabled us to establish a presence in Asian aerospace markets, by co-funding Interturbine Singapore.

Meanwhile, the modern venture capital industry was taking shape, with George Doriot as a linchpin. Indivers benefited from the network of firms that emerged, both in the U.S. and Europe.

Doriot founded one of the first venture capital firms in the U.S., American Research and Development Corporation (ARD). ARD is renowned for its $70,000 investment in Digital Equipment Corporation in 1957, which was valued at over $355 million after the company's initial public offering (IPO) in 1968. ARD also supported Indivers.

Doriot also founded Europe's first venture capital firm, Paris-based European Enterprise Development (EED), in 1971. Indivers was one of its early investments. When EED was unable to raise additional funds and closed a few years later, its 10% share in Indivers was purchased by Palmer, an ARD spin-off in Boston. That introduced us to Steve Ricci, a Palmer partner, who became a key member of our board.

"What about angel investors, or public markets?" I am sometimes asked. Angel investors were not part of the formal financial scene for most of Indivers' history, but now are an important source of capital for entrepreneurs.[15] Public markets did emerge in Europe, during Indivers' history, but I wanted to remain privately held. (More on that in Chapter 6.)

Indivers' joint ventures

Many of Indivers' early start-ups were through joint ventures with industry partners, financial institutions, or research groups. It was totally opportunistic, and all on a personal basis. A manager would make a contact with someone who had either technology or market access of interest to us, and I would get involved.

Walbar is an interesting example of partnering, for both technology and market access.

In 1973, we came across a company called Walbar (in Peabody, Massachusetts) that was an expert at servicing stationary turbines. We did a joint venture to bring the technology into Indivers, and called it Elbar. After a while, Walbar backed out;

---

[15] For more information about angel investing, see Financing High-Growth Firms: The Role of Angel Investors, OECD Publishing, 2011. http://dx.doi.org/10.1787/9789264118782-en

the start-up costs were too high for them. We soldiered on, developing the technology on our own.

Elbar became a success by servicing power stations in developing markets. The average station has only one or two turbine engines (worth $50-100 million each), not enough for an in-house service crew. Except for the U.S., stations did not have access to contract service providers. We went into the Middle East and India, and filled the void. (That's why we had an Iranian manager and a Palestinian sales manager.)

In total, Indivers was involved in 25 joint ventures, in nine countries, over the years. (See Exhibit 5-6)

I learned the hard way, by being forced out of Aluminium Extruders by my majority partner, to insist on at least a 50% share of each joint venture. In most cases, we bought out our partner, or our partner exited for its own strategic reasons. There were a few failures, usually due to partner impatience for results.

One partnership stands out as a glaring exception to Indivers' typical joint venture approach: the PW4000 project.

In the early 1980s, Indivers was presented with a unique opportunity: a Pratt & Whitney project to develop its next generation of engines. The PW4000 project was huge, expected to cost $3 billion and take 5-10 years for completion. The engines would sell for $10 million each, with the total market value estimated at $70 billion, at the time.[16]

Engine manufacturers routinely formed partnerships with a number of industry players, to fund such large projects. We already had a relationship with P&W, and they proposed that we become a 1% risk partner, along with global players like

---

[16] In 2013, the market has already exceeded $80 billion. Including spare parts, it could ultimately reach $300 billion.

MTU Germany and Samsung Korea. It was a great chance to elevate Indivers' visibility.

Our 1% partnership would cost us $30 million. As a risk partner, we would get exclusive rights to manufacture 500 out of the engine's 25,000 parts over the 40-year life of the engine, at a nice margin. We estimated the value of the business to Indivers at $700 million. It all sounded good, except that we only had $10 million.

We were able to finance the rest through the Netherlands government and banks, to be repaid within 10 years. In 1986, Indivers and the banks set up Finco as an off-balance sheet financial vehicle (i.e., it did not appear in our numbers) for the arrangement, and handed over $30 million to P&W.

Shortly afterwards, P&W asked its partners for an additional $1 billion, our 1% share coming to $10 million. Then came an airline industry crisis, resulting in a sales slow-down and delay of full production, and huge discounting by P&W to sell the new engine. As risk partner, we felt those losses, too.

Our bank partners were unwilling to move forward. We dissolved Finco in 1990, and got out of the risk partnership with P&W. The banks took a big loss, as did Indivers. The Belgian and Norwegian partners in the project went bust.

Then – surprise! - P&W offered us an exclusive manufacturing partnership, at a lower margin. We gladly accepted, knowing that we could still make good money. The project became the mainstay of Interturbine's business, and will be making good money for Interturbine's acquirer until at least 2034.

It was a stressful experience, but with a happy ending; a good way to end this chapter!

EXHIBIT 5-1

Indivers' research network

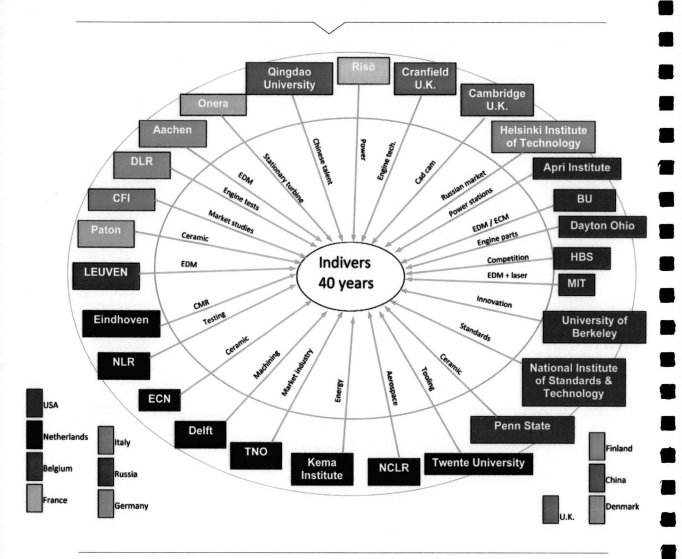

EXHIBIT 5-2

Indivers' university student network

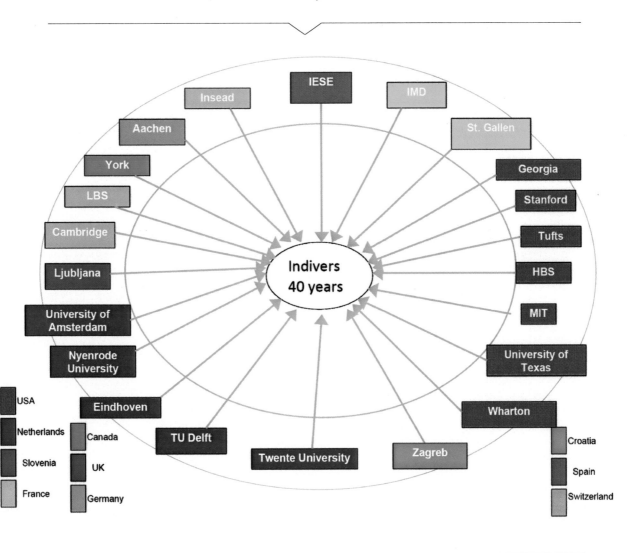

EXHIBIT 5-3

Indivers' managers

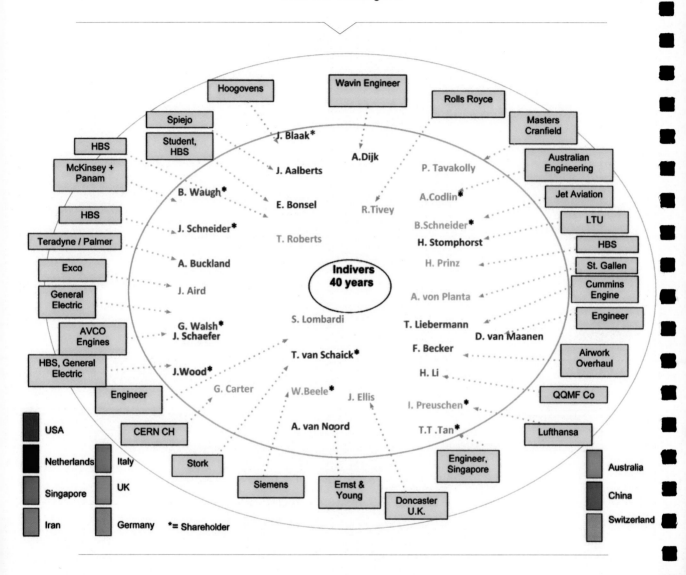

EXHIBIT 5-4

Indivers' board members

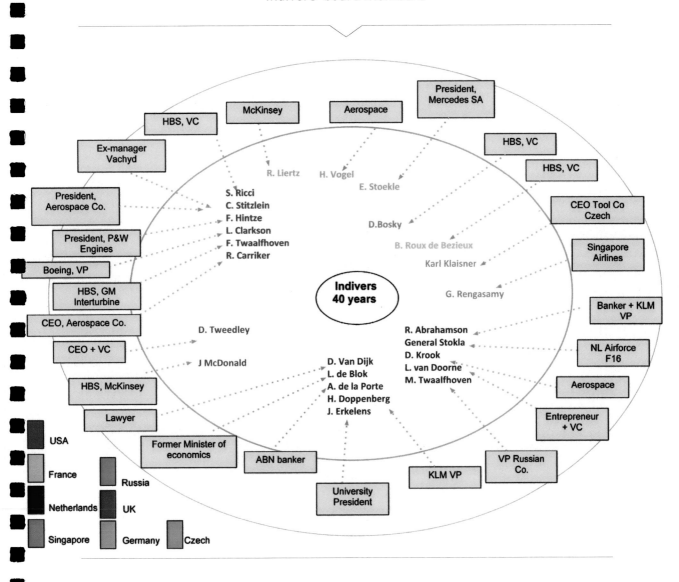

EXHIBIT 5-5

Indivers' financial network

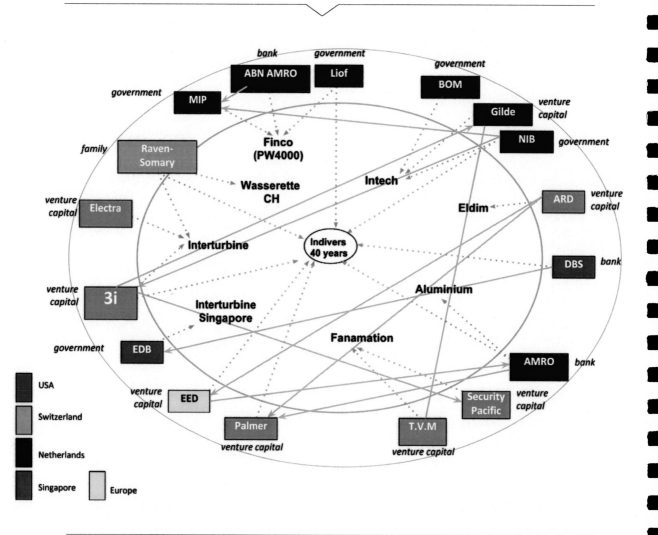

EXHIBIT 5-6

Indivers' joint ventures

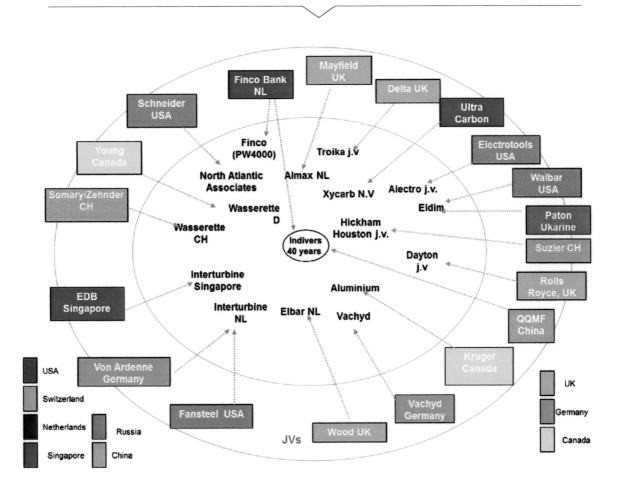

CHAPTER 6

Managing growth:
Professional intrapreneurship

Take another look at that cyclone of Indivers' growth, at the beginning of Chapter 2.

How do you manage that? How can you keep up fast-paced growth, without spinning out of control? How can you get bigger, without getting bureaucratic?

The answer is what I call "professional intrapreneurship." That sounds like an oxymoron, I know. How can an organization be disciplined and entrepreneurial, at the same time?

In the following sections, we'll look at some key elements of the approach we used at Indivers, and how the organization evolved as we grew and changed. I'll also share some observations about family and business.

Management structure

My thinking about how to organize Indivers was influenced by some research on our competitors. I was impressed by the decentralized approach used by Chromollay, a turbine competitor. (I also recalled, from my HBS days, that it was the approach used by Textron.) That meant autonomous units, very lean corporate staff, and as little as possible in between.

Indivers' decentralized holding company model had a number of advantages, for professional intrapreneurship: flexibility to add (and subtract) businesses, few layers to slow communication and decision-making, central oversight and resource allocation, and opportunities for entrepreneurial managers to flourish.

Each niche that Indivers entered became a profit centre, with a balance sheet, P&L statement, and a local banker. They were small, ranging from 25 to several hundred people. Managers had a lot of autonomy, if they were performing to objectives. My philosophy: leave them alone when they're making money, and get intensely involved when things go bad.

Each profit centre was expected to make it on its own and grow, with support from a very lean but dedicated corporate staff, and – if a sufficiently strong business case could be made – Indivers risk capital. Our managers typically were young, and technically proficient in their tooling specialty.

For the first decade or so, I was mainly focused on Wasserette, while Jan Aalberts, as COO, oversaw the Almax companies. Our controller, Wim Visser, handled all personnel and administrative activities at headquarters, which was a 17th century office in Amsterdam.[17] We added a business development manager, to look for more tooling opportunities.

By the mid-1970s, we needed help managing our now 16 business units, in four countries. We created four divisions, along our expanded product lines, and began recruiting managers from top business schools, as well as large industry players and competitors.

The division structure would shift a few times, as Indivers continued to expand geographically, and build the turbine business. It was trial and error, to some degree. For example, when we acquired VacHyd, we split our turbine operations into a U.S. division, and another Holland-based division for other geographies, each with a CEO. When the U.S. business faltered, we recentralized.

Another example: as we became more involved in the turbine industry, we saw that there were major differences between the flying and stationary sides of the business, strategically and operationally. Aviation customers were more demanding, with much more stringent quality control requirements. We split Interturbine into separate divisions.

---

[17] We would relocate to larger headquarters facilities, in later years.

Over time, we began to professionalize our senior management, looking for top talent. Tom Liebermann, who was recruited for business development in 1983, offers this perspective on the shift:

I believe that there are entrepreneurs and re-entrepreneurs. You need both, in a growing enterprise. Entrepreneurs are usually early stage, green field. They are very broad and curious. When they see something, they'll go after it. Bert is a born entrepreneur. A re-entrepreneur is about doing better, about innovation to get to the next level. Both are important, at different stages.

I am a re-entrepreneur. When I arrived, Indivers was 20 companies, a collection of cats and dogs. Bert handed me a stack of documents and said: "What's our strategy?" Within a year and a half, we had a coherent strategy that the board loved. And, any acquisition had to pass the test question: how does it fit? It was about Indivers' second stage; about turbo-charging.

As Interturbine became increasingly important to Indivers, we set up a separate subsidiary for it, with its own CEO and board. We felt that the move would provide business focus and help us attract the leadership talent we needed, allowing me to begin stepping back from operations. It worked: Gordon Walsh agreed to take the CEO position, in 1996.

People and culture

Indivers' growth was more constrained by the ability to find human than financial resources.

As we saw in Chapter 5, building networks of external partners and recruiting management talent was one of my most important roles, as founder and owner. Setting the right tone for organization was another; I tried to practice rather than preach the kind of behaviours that I expected.

> *Bert wasn't about grand strategies or value statements. He led by example, through the hundreds of little decisions he made every day. It's possible to lead that way, but every little signal has to be consistent. It's like a jazz quintet. Bert had a clear set of values. There was a line in the sand, and you didn't want to cross it. He was a tough business-man, but he didn't have a mean bone in his body. He was simple and straightforward in his business dealings, which is very Dutch.*
>
> *- Art Buckland*

We were constantly on the lookout for the right talent, through personal contacts and executive search firms. One way we were able to attract more talent than you might expect, for a company our size, was by serving as a school for entrepreneurs. Indivers was remarkable for the sheer number of young people we hired, and the encouragement they received to be entrepreneurial. Steve Ricci recalls:

The pursuit of opportunities and "managing beyond your resources" were instilled as part of the culture. Everyone came up with ideas. Rather than say "no," we would sort them out. Managers were always lobbying for money for new equipment or expansion, but also were out looking for development funds and partners.

We never felt we "owned" our managers, and even helped some fund their own start-ups. I am very proud of the 36 Indivers managers who went on to become entrepreneurs in their own rights. (See Exhibit 6-1)

We were resistant to any hints of bureaucracy, even as Indivers grew and "professionalized." Tom Liebermann, who came to Indivers from a Fortune 500 company, particularly appreciated our entrepreneurial culture:

One of Indivers' huge assets was speed, of operations, data, and decision-making. If I wanted to make a decision, I'd just make the decision. If I needed information, I'd go talk to a business unit head. We'd do one analysis for an acquisition. We had monthly management meetings. There weren't ten levels to wade through.

Another of our strengths was the mix of experience and youth: old timers and hare-brained freshmen. You'd go to the old British guy from Rolls Royce, puffing on his pipe, and he'd say: "You can't do that in aerospace because..." Then you'd get someone like me saying: "Why can't it be done?" It's about the importance of confrontation, and the absence of politics.

Planning

Planning was an important discipline at Indivers, and I have given many talks on business planning and entrepreneurial finance, over the years.

> *When Bert got his MBA, the financial analysis and planning methods that he knew were unique in Europe, aside from Shell. Even in 1983, when I got my business degree and was looking for work in Europe, the skill-set obtained with an MBA from Harvard was only properly utilized and rewarded by larger American companies operating in Europe.*
>
> *- Felix Twaalfhoven*

One of my complaints is that business schools, even now, often don't teach how to understand the numbers, from the perspective of a smaller business. Corporate finance and entrepreneurial finance are different, in theory and practice. For an entrepreneur, cash flow is king, the timing of financing is critical, and capital markets often are inaccessible and unorganized.

"The failure of business plans" is a related complaint, and a frequent talk theme. The failure stems from two commonly held myths: that you can get rich quick; and that you can get it right the first time.

"Hockey stick" charts - much beloved by aspiring entrepreneurs – illustrate both myths. The charts typically show revenue, customers, cash, or some other measure increasing dramatically at some point in the future.[18] The curve at the bottom is sometimes called "the valley of death;" if you don't have enough cash to make it through, you're a goner.

Steve Ricci, with the benefit of his venture capitalist experience, sums up the problem beautifully:

Nearly all business plans, entrepreneurs and managers underestimate risks, and the time required to identify and react to them. Time is the biggest enemy to a company that is losing money, because the risks encountered always require more time, and it's hard to secure resources on favourable terms when some of the negative realities have emerged. As a result, many ventures succumb to financial difficulties, or the founder and early investors enjoy a severely diminished share of the pie.

I routinely caution entrepreneurs about the dangers of unrealistic planning. One year, we distributed miniature field hockey sticks with "Indivers budget" lettered on the side, to all our managers. They got the message: no overly rosy predictions, please.

Budgeting and forecasting are just the first, critical steps. An agile organization with a learning attitude will continually iterate their assumptions, to reflect the impact of reality.

- Art Buckland

If you're starting a business, you'll need five-year financing. But you can't wait for that, so don't stop for a minute. Implement and execute, and be prepared to scrounge for money.

- Tom Liebermann

---

[18] The name comes from the almost 90 degree change in the graph's line when initially low results suddenly shoot up.

When giving talks, I sometimes share the results of a study that looked at the business planning and risk capital experiences of 200 start-ups, including Indivers. The study's conclusion: it takes five years, and multiple iterations of your business plan, to make money. (See Exhibit 6-2 for study highlights)

The reality is that a start-up, by definition, is dealing with the unknown. No matter how carefully you plan, you won't really know until you try. The one thing that you can count on is that there will be setbacks. Another challenge facing most entrepreneurs: unless you are independently wealthy, you're going to have to get financing.

At Indivers, each business unit manager prepared a five-year plan (by year) in September, and an annual budget (by month) by year end. The plans weren't just an extrapolation from current year; they had to reflect a review of actuals, previous year performance, and explain the assumptions behind future projections.

During planning meetings, I would ask things like: How long will it take to prove the technology, and get market acceptance? How many customers do you have? If you have a delay, what will the financial impact be? What if you're sick for eight weeks?

The point was to get managers to step back and ask themselves: "What could go wrong? And, if it does, what are some options for solving the problem?"

I call that *negative business planning*. At Indivers, it was required. As an angel investor, I am reassured when an aspiring entrepreneur presents this sort of reality check, and tend to be more understanding when and if he comes back for more money.

Risk capital is an on-going challenge, for a growth company. You have options: generate it internally or tap into private or public markets. Steve Ricci explains an important trade-off:

As an entrepreneur, you have to be clear about your objectives: do you want to be a large company with outside capital? If not, you have to adjust your goals, and generate capital other ways. Bert liked capital partners, but didn't like the constraints that go with them. He relied on retained earnings, seldom issuing dividends. He also used debt more than most companies, to finance growth. He was reluctant to give up control and privacy.

In the early 1980s, we cleaned ourselves up for a possible IPO, selling some underperforming assets, checking out various stock exchanges, and writing a prospectus that positioned Indivers as "an advanced technology window into Europe, into the world." We ultimately decided to stay private. It was a useful exercise, though, and helped us with some important private placements, a few years later.

Management controls

At Indivers, our management control systems provided a continuous flow of information about our operational and financial performance.

Every Monday, from all over the world, our office in Amsterdam would receive figures on incoming orders and production deliveries for the past week. (And remember, that was without computers, in the early days!) We wanted no surprises. If no data arrived, we expected that something was wrong and the manager would do something about it. If nothing happened in three days, he'd get a call.

On the first day of the month, sales estimates came in, and within five working days of the new month, we got order data and P&L estimates from each plant, for the previous month. I was able to get information from China, even during the big Tet holidays.

Personally, that meant daily communications –faxes, phone calls, and emails – even when I was skiing or sailing with the family and friends. (That was irritating to many people, I know!)

We also required monthly balance sheets, income statements, and reports on personnel levels and cash flows. The Group Committee (myself and division managers) met each month, to talk about progress against the annual plan, progress against the five-year plan, and long-term directions. Mid-year, we would make adjustments to plans, as necessary.

Indivers' incentive systems were designed to keep us focused on results. Company managers' bonuses were a percentage of their unit profits. Division managers were evaluated and rewarded based on profit performance against budget. They received a bonus on division profits, and overall company results; several received Indivers stock options. Key corporate staff also received bonus and stock incentives.

Crisis management

These days, "crisis management" often connotes an expensive public relations effort, to smooth over a disaster. (Remember the 2010 oil spill in the Gulf of Mexico, when BP's CEO Tony Hayward made the unfortunate error of downplaying the problem, and saying that he "wanted his life back?")

For an entrepreneur, crises are to be expected, and you do not have the luxury of passing it on to someone else. "The buck stops here," is the unavoidable reality. At Indivers, we had more than 40 crises, over as many years. We've seen several of them, in previous chapters; Exhibit 6-3 shares a few more illustrative examples.

Why so many? There are limits to formal controls and incentives, for one thing. The unexpected will arise, no matter how tightly you manage. For another, Indivers' decentralized and geographically disbursed organization meant that we depended on the integrity - as well as the talent – of managers on the front lines.

The key to dealing with crises is to be able to size up the situation quickly, and tap into your networks to come up with creative solutions. Perhaps most important: do something, fast, and if that doesn't work, try something else. Sound stressful? It is. Sometimes you are successful, and sometimes you are not.

Family and business

I began thinking about the company as a family business early on, with the Brenninkmeijer family as a role model. (They asked me to work for them, after HBS, but

I wanted my independence.) The Brenninkmeijers had built a retail empire, C&A, with multiple generations involved in the business. Career paths were carefully planned, and family members picked leadership successors.

I also had learned at HBS that 80% of start-ups and companies are family run. Multi-generational family businesses, though, have always been rare. "Shirt sleeves to shirt sleeves in three generations" is the American version of a proverb with variations around the world; most family businesses don't survive the first generation.

But, I was undaunted, thinking that my children – at least some of them – would take over the helm, when it was time for me to step down. I consulted some family business experts, about how to prepare the family for business.

In 1977, we started having annual family meetings at different Indivers locations around the world. Each family member would talk about his or her goals and plans, and we would get reports on the business. Indivers board members, managers, and advisors also attended. We held 27 consecutive meetings.

I also was advised to give my children direct exposure to the business. Each of them worked at Indivers or its subsidiaries for periods as short as six months, and as long as 15 years. They held various positions: market research, business development, IT support, factory management, and division management. Towards the end, two became board members.

By the mid-1990s, I had realized that family succession probably was not in the cards, for Indivers. I wanted to give my children the opportunity to carry on the family business, but not force it on them. They had their own interests, and could handle their own destinies.

The Twaalfhoven share of proceeds from Interturbine's sale was put in a trust that was distributed among family members. Today, six of my children are entrepreneurs in their own right, and two are independently involved in philanthropic ventures.

If you asked my eight children and my wife, Maria, to comment on Indivers as a family business, you probably would get nine different stories. I won't go that far, but will share one version, from my son Felix:

We all worked at Indivers at some point, but none of us wanted to stay. One reason was the nature of the industry. Indivers operating companies primarily repaired and manufactured metal components used in turbine engines. The typical staff consisted of welders, machinists, and management with an industrial background.

The second reason was Indivers' holding company structure. There was factory level, where you could be an engineer or manager, but promotion could only go up to one spot – CEO of Indivers, and Bert made it clear that he was not about to retire. There were few opportunities in between.

What Indivers did allow was an infrastructure from which we, as the children, could start our own companies, in industries that were more interesting to us. It was the Internet Age, so software was a popular choice, and two of my brothers pursued that path. Another started a company making measurement robotics; one of Indivers' companies became a client. The youngest brother was a top university soccer player, and opened a chain of fitness clubs.

Indivers was the family's major asset, and the money was always reinvested. It wasn't a cash machine, but it did provide family-enjoyable assets, like "company" sailboats, an apartment in Boston, and a chalet in Switzerland. Times have changed, though. Today, you couldn't have those assets on your balance sheet.

Family business or entrepreneurial family? In our case, the latter, I think.

EXHIBIT 6-1

Indivers managers who became entrepreneurs

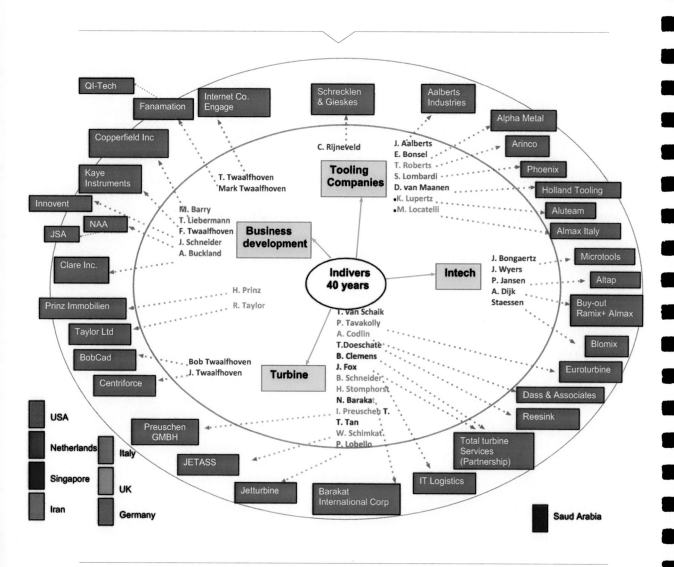

Source: "Becoming a Global Entrepreneur: It Takes Networks, Passion, Failures, and Experience,"
S. Vyakarnam and Y Myint, Centre for Entrepreneurial Learning, Judge Business School, University of Cambridge, 2006.

EXHIBIT 6-2

Business planning and risk capital study[19]

Conclusion: It takes five years, and multiple plans, to make money.

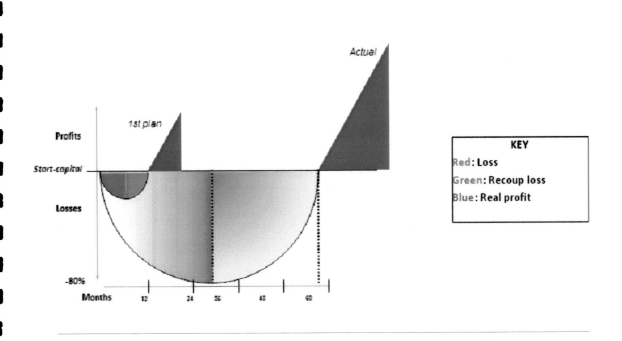

KEY	
Red: **Loss**	
Green: **Recoup loss**	
Blue: **Real profit**	

Business plan #1. You need a $2 million capital investment. You can fund part of it, and your family funds the rest, for 25% ownership. Losses are projected to bottom out at $700,000 after 6 months, and be recouped in 12 months. Ten months later, you've accumulated losses of $1.5 million, and your timetable is in trouble. Product development has been delayed, due to technical problems.

[19] Source: Indivers hired two HBS students to analyse the portfolio of a Chicago venture-capital company and Indivers own experience. Professor Jack Timmons incorporated the results in a discussion of start-ups in his book, New Venture Creation.

Business plan #2. You'll need an additional $1 million of capital, which you can get from an angel investing group but at a cost; your ownership drops to 50%. You expect losses to stop in two months, and be recouped at Month 24 of the project. After eighteen months, losses have mounted to $2.5 million. Market penetration has been slower than expected.

Business plan #3. You'll need another $1 million. The family backs out, but you're able to get a venture capital firm and bank to invest. Your ownership drops to 28%. You expect losses to stop in two more months, and be recouped at Month 36. Thirty months into the project, losses are at $3.5 million. There's been a management shakeup at your company. Some key team mates have quit, and strategic partners (e.g., distributors) are about to go.

Business plan #4. Another $1 million needed, for total capitalization of $5 million. Your new projections – losses stopped at Month 34 and recouped at Month 58 - will prove close to actual. The angel investors back out. The venture capitalist/bank consortium becomes your sole partner, for 88% ownership. You will not survive.

EXHIBIT 6-3

A sampling of Indivers' 42 crises in 42 years

Farmer walks out. I help a Dutch family emigrate to work on my dairy farm in Quebec. I move back to Holland, and learn that they have purchased their own farm, and are selling my herd.

Factory shut down by court. Aluminium Extruders cancels its orders with a tool supplier, due to quality problems. They claim that we are contractually obligated, and get a court order shutting us down.

Company buyer disappears. I negotiate the sale of the Wasserette Company. The buyer signs 36 months of payment instalment cheques, and then disappears. All the cheques bounce.

Company manager disappears. One Monday morning, the Almax Paris manager closes the factory door and leaves, stealing a company car. Workers have been fired, and there are two large dogs in the yard.

Shareholder goes bankrupt. Venture capital firm with 10% of Indivers shares fails, and offers the shares on the stock market, without our knowledge.

Employee theft. I get a call during dinner from our CEO: "The bookkeeper has stolen the company credit card, and spent 10,000 guilders over two days." Two hours later, I learn that the amount actually is 75,000 guilders - $30,000 - spent at three night clubs in Dusseldorf.

Workers go on strike. Communist cell at our Almax Italy factory go on strike demanding equal pay for all workers, regardless of years of employment and experience.

Joint venture partner quits. Walbar Massachusetts partner quits, leaving us to absorb three-year start-up losses plus loss of technology and market acceptance.

Cyanide in toilets. Cynanide from a treatment process used at a plant in Los

Angeles escapes to residential area, through the sewage system.

Company manager dying. On Christmas Day, I get a call from Interturbine's CEO (who oversees 12 companies): "Please come to Boston. It's urgent." I arrive the next day. He's been diagnosed with cancer; four months to live.

Employee fraud. A former Interturbine bookkeeper informs us that the Dallas manager has been overstating inventory - $3 million over two years, undetected by the auditors – just as we're signing the PW4000 risk partner agreement with Pratt & Whitney.

Partner give-away. A government venture capital entity demands more shares of Indivers if we don't make the next year's budget, which would effectively give it a blocking minority position.

Bad publicity. A Washington DC lobbyist firm called "Rent a General" gets bad publicity. Indivers is one of its clients.

Five-year planning meeting with Division Presidents and Board of Directors
(Bert is front, left) at Indivers headquarters in Amsterdam, 1976.

Board meeting in 1980
(with Bert standing in the middle)

From foreground, clockwise: Bob Twaalfhoven
(CAD/CAM specialist), Tom Liebermann
(Business Development), Gerald Carter
(President Intech Division), 1985.

107

Four of the 34 Indivers managers who became entrepreneurs. From top left, clockwise:
Jan Aalberts, Aalberts Industries, NL; Ellen Bonsel, Alpha Metal, NL;
Mark Twaalfhoven; Fanamation Inc. USA
Burckhard Schneider, Interturbine Logistics, Germany.

The Board and management, and their partners , 1996 (with Bert on left).

Board meeting with new Interturbine CEO Gordon Walsh,
1996 (with Bert on the left).

The Twaalfhoven children, all grown up 2010.

CHAPTER 7

Giving back:
Easy, satisfying, and a responsibility

There are three myths about "giving back" that I'd like to dispel, to start.

First, it's not all about money. We each have many gifts to offer. Time, knowledge, skills, experience, networks, and encouragement are all tremendously valuable resources. (Money is nice, too, though.)

Second, it is something that you can do early, and often. It's not about one grand gesture, when you have "made it." There are many small ways you can make a difference, all along the way.

Last but not least, it's not a one-way street. It is so satisfying, to be able to help one person achieve his goals, or contribute to a cause that you believe in.

Each person must set his own priorities for giving. In my case, they are international education, and entrepreneurship.

You'll see those themes throughout this chapter, as we look at my experiences giving back.

My alma maters

I am grateful to Fordham University and Harvard Business School for investing in me and my future, through over six years of scholarships. At Harvard, where so many talented students have received support, you learn that alumni are part of the process, and are expected to give back generously.

At Fordham, I participate in alumni giving programs, and have served on its International Advisory Board and Finance Visiting Committee. In 2003, we established The Bert Twaalfhoven Center for Entrepreneurship, which encourages the development of family businesses and social entrepreneurship, while preparing budding entrepreneurs with the skills to start their own businesses.

I am a grateful donor to HBS as well, and active in alumni affairs. In 1971, HBS decided to set up an alumni club in Europe, and made me the head. It was an opportunity to meet business leaders from all across Europe. We met annually, each year at a different university, for programs with HBS professors.

In 1982, HBS asked me to serve as head of the worldwide alumni group. An opportunity to meet business leaders from across the globe! Every door opened. I found myself giving Steve Jobs of Apple a prize, with Arthur Rock, a leading venture capitalist.

HBS also was breaking ground in the field of entrepreneurship in the early 1980s, having realized that almost half of its graduates would become entrepreneurs, at some point in their careers. With Arthur Rock's generous support, a new academic centre for entrepreneurial management was created, with Professor Howard Stevenson at its helm.

It was the start of ground breaking work that led to the conclusion that entrepreneurship was less about the person, and more about a process that could be learned and taught. It was exciting to be in the thick of it, invited to the centre's first symposium, and eager to spread the word to Europe.

Meanwhile, my European campaign for entrepreneurship was already underway.

Entrepreneurship in Europe

In the 1970s, Professor David Birch's research at the Massachusetts Institute of Technology was showing that small, high growth businesses (gazelles, he dubbed them) were creating new jobs and driving employment growth in the U.S.; not large, established firms (elephants) or corner stores (mice).

That caught the attention of some policymakers in Europe, as well as the U.S.

With McKinsey's support, I arranged for Birch to visit Europe. Partly because of that, and partly because Indivers qualified as a gazelle, people considered me a credible spokesperson for entrepreneurship.

I was asked to serve on a number of initiatives, including a commission to advise government on how to provide more risk capital for start-ups, and a project for industrial innovation. The World Small Business Council invited me to join as the Dutch delegate. That role took me to Kuala Lumpur, Malaga, Washington DC, Warsaw, and beyond, providing great insight into international business.

Still, I was stunned when the World Economic Forum asked me to be a panellist at its annual meeting in 1985, in Davos, Switzerland.[20] The panel was called "The Spirit of Entrepreneurship." It would be chaired by Raymond Barre, the former Prime Minister of France. My co-panelists would be the CEO of IBM, John Akers, and the Governor of Germany, Lothar Spath.

Bert Twaalfhoven with John Akers, on the same stage? Unbelievable!

An audience of over 1,000 people was expected. Wanting to do a good job, I hired Neil Smith, an HBS student who was a former Financial Times journalist, to help me prepare. We started with a picture of Gulliver (that would be IBM) and the little people (that would be the entrepreneurs). That got a laugh.

My talk highlighted the importance of small business for job creation, the challenges facing entrepreneurs, and the role of institutions and society in promoting entrepreneurship. It closed with a series of recommendations that – looking back at them – remain sound even today.

I was inspired to go the next step in promoting entrepreneurship in Europe, with the help of John McDonald (my classmate at HBS, and EFER co-founder). He recalls:

[20] The World Economic Forum is an independent international organization committed to improving the state of the world by engaging business, political, academic and other leaders to shape global, regional and industry agendas.

CHAPTER 7

We looked at the US experience, and found that successful entrepreneurs had a number of things in common. Many had been to business schools, and studied all the basic management functions. They vetted themselves, figuring out what they were good at, and then building a team of people with other expertise. They spread ownership and responsibilities right. They lost money to begin with, and took a while to get in the black. We did some interviews in Europe, talking to business people and academics. We found that entrepreneurship studies at European business schools, at best, consisted of no more than a one-week course, and were focused on American rather than European success stories.

In the fall of 1986, we formed a task force to discuss the founding of an institution that would take a Europe-wide approach to entrepreneurism, with a focus on emerging growth firms. The time seemed right, with the prospect of the European Union in 1992. (Little did we know that the Berlin Wall would fall, and the Soviet Bloc dismantle before then!)

EFER

In 1987, we established a nonprofit organization to foster new research on emerging growth firms, develop mechanisms for interaction, and identify barriers and obstacles to growth. The European Forum for Entrepreneurship Research (EFER) was born, with a small headquarters office in Brussels.

We decided to start by offering opportunities to professors to do research on successful European entrepreneurs, and holding a conference to share results. We were able to assemble a group of interested sponsors, including McKinsey and Arthur Andersen, the EVCA (European Venture Capital Association), the EFMD (European Foundation for Management Development), and some entrepreneurs and venture capitalists.

In 2012, EFER celebrated its twenty-fifth anniversary. It's been an exciting journey. EFER's "Europe-wide" scope has expanded to include Eastern and Western

Europe. We also have broadened and deepened our support for entrepreneurship education, and actively pursued efforts to engage business leaders and entrepreneurs.

Entrepreneurship education

Entrepreneurship was the exception, not the rule, in many European universities, when EFER started. Over the years, we have adopted a three-pronged effort to address that challenge: faculty training and development, curriculum and course material development, and cross-border faculty collaboration and exchange.

During the 1990s, we sponsored a series of case research projects, held annual conferences, and conducted workshops on how to write and teach case studies. We adopted a "teach-the-teacher" approach that leverages impact, as each professor can then train multiple groups of students over many years. We also had our first EFER network meetings, bringing together faculty from many countries.

In 2004, I engaged HBS alumnae Karen Wilson, now executive director of EFER, to help develop our strategy going forward. As part of that process, we conducted a survey of entrepreneurship education in Europe that identified a number of important trends. Karen highlights the key findings:

The survey showed that entrepreneurship education was starting to grow significantly in Europe, however, it was still relatively new and housed mostly in business schools or economics departments, instead of integrated across the curriculum in all disciplines. (Entrepreneurs come from many backgrounds, particularly from science and technology.)

Second, there was a need not only for training but also networks and support mechanisms for entrepreneurship professors in Europe, as the field was still young and many professors felt like lone rangers in their institutions. Finally, we found that the majority of entrepreneurship professors taught in their home countries, and needed greater international experience.

The survey captured the attention of policy makers, universities and professors across Europe; and reinforced the importance of EFER's work. We decided to intensify our training efforts.

Following a 2001 pilot program at Cambridge University, HBS generously co-hosted EECPCL (European Entrepreneurship Colloquium on Participant-Centered Learning) programs in Boston for four years. An eight-day intensive residential experience, EECPCL was for faculty who would be leading curriculum development and research in their home institutions.

In 2009, the program returned to Europe as the European Entrepreneurship Colloquium (EEC). It now is held annually at a different university, in a different country, with international faculty participants and facilitators. The European Commission has been a co-sponsor since 2010. Other partners have included the University of Cambridge, IESE Business School (in Spain), the Warsaw School of Economics, Ozyegin (in Istanbul), Leuven (In Belgium), and TUM (in Munich).

As of 2012, 456 professors from 183 institutions in 43 European countries have been trained by EFER.

In addition, EFER hosts alumni roundtable meetings to provide a platform for continued learning, networking, and exchange of practices. EFER has also piloted a cross-border faculty exchange program, and supported the development of over 50 case studies and 40 research publications, for use by academics as well as policy makers.

Reaching and engaging entrepreneurs

In 1995, EFER was approached by the EU commissioner with a question: how to find Europe's gazelles? Big business and SMEs were well represented in EU organizations; dynamic entrepreneurs were not. We were eager to respond, and then go a step further by connecting entrepreneurship academics with real-world practitioners.

EFER launched a study to target dynamic entrepreneurs. We also knew that Ernst & Young (E&Y) had launched an "Entrepreneur of the Year" program in the U.S., in partnership with INC Magazine. We invited the EU, E&Y, the EU, Dun & Bradstreet, and the European Venture Capital Organization (EVCO) to introduce the program to Europe. In 1996, we jointly established "Europe's 500," to find and honour European gazelles.

E&Y subsequently expanded its Entrepreneur of the Year program globally. Europe's 500 publishes a list of high growth European companies, and sponsors an "Entrepreneurship Growth Summit" annually. In addition to recognizing dynamic entrepreneurs and providing opportunities to network, it lobbies on behalf of entrepreneurs on issues of interest to them.

EFER has launched a research project called the New European Champions, to develop case studies on successful entrepreneurs from Central and Eastern Europe. We also have sponsored a study looking at how universities spin off technology and science-based businesses. Study participants include four European schools (Cambridge University, UK; KU Leuven, Belgium; ETH Zurich, Switzerland; TU Munich, Germany).

We also are exploring new ways to encourage greater interaction between academics and "real world" practitioners, through entrepreneur-in-residence programs.

Looking to the future

Much has been accomplished, but much remains to be done, and EFER is excited to play a leading role. As our scope and impact grows, we also must address the challenge of ensuring EFER's sustainability and leadership.

The EFER organization currently consists of a small core team, with the support and guidance of two important bodies: an international Board of Directors, and a group of Academic Advisors from U.S. and European schools. In 2013, we will be forming a Board of International Entrepreneurs to advise us on current issues for practitioners, and help us set EFER's project priorities.

I am extremely proud of the entire EFER community, and the work we do, and invite you to learn more about us at www.efer.eu.

Now, an important point: You do not have to start a foundation to have an impact on your community. You can make a difference, all through your career, and be the better for it.

Giving and getting

As a business owner, you have an opportunity to help talented young people. At Indivers, we hired many students as summer interns, and were able to help some of them obtain scholarships for MBA studies. Some returned as permanent employees. Indivers also was a training ground for managers who went on to become entrepreneurs themselves.

You also can contribute by sharing your business acumen. I have served on company boards, and participate in angel investing, not as "charity," but as a way to help entrepreneurs with good ideas succeed. My business skills have proven useful to non-profits that I support, including United World Colleges, several Dutch museums, and Atalya (a Dutch missionary agricultural school) in Panama.

Telling the Indivers story has been another way to give back. It is great fun having a dialogue with my audiences. I have given over 260 talks worldwide, to university professors and students, business school alumni, government and public policy groups, rotary groups, and organizations promoting entrepreneurship. Indivers also has been the subject of four business school case studies.[21]

---

[21] Wasserette by Vincent Jolivet, IMD, 1970s; INDIVERS NV by Philippe Haspeslach, Insead 1983 and Stanford 1985; QI-Tech: A Chinese Technology Company for Sale by Walter Kuemmerle, HBS 2004 (revised); Bert Twaalfhoven: The Successes and Failures of a Global Entrepreneur by Daniel Isenberg, HBS 2008.

There has been some formal recognition of my contributions, including an honorary doctoral degree from Fordham, and an alumni achievement award from HBS. The importance, to me, of those awards is that they acknowledged my efforts to advance international entrepreneurism. That is immensely satisfying.

My support for my alma maters and entrepreneurship was not commercially motivated. But, it did give me – and by extension – Indivers visibility and credibility. (How else could I have got the head of a university, a former Minister of Economicas, a former Board member of Mercedes, and a Senior Vice President of Boeing to join me – a farmer turned industrialist - on my board?!)

The best payback, though, has been the opportunity to meet so many committed and talented people, many of whom have become friends. Thank you, all.

Bert at the 1985 W orld Economic Forum, on a "Small is Beautiful" panel with (left to right) John Aker, president of IBM; Raymond Baar, President France; and Lothar Spät, German Parliament member

Peter Drucker and Bert (on the right) at a panel for the European Management Association, 1982

David Birch of MIT

Honorary PhD degree from Fordham, 1985. (Bert is top right)

HBS Alumni Achievement Award 2011 Bert, Dean Kim Clark, former Dean John McArthur

EFER's first colloquium for European professors, at HBS, in 2005.

Europe's 500 inaugural event, honouring Europe's growth entrepreneurs 1995.

Bert with Karen Wilson (EFER Executive Director), and Howard Stevenson (HBS professor and EFER supporter)

New European Champions, Warsaw Colloquium, 2011

Tea Petrin, EFER Academic Advisor, University of Ljubljana professor.

Bert's LEARN EARN RETURN book co-author, Shirley Spence

BT giving a talk, using one of his LER favourite slides: a mother bird feeding her young. (Give back)

Conclusion:
A Call to action

Dynamic entrepreneurship creates jobs and drives economic growth, as well as serving as a wellspring of innovation to meet society's needs. That is a powerful and hopeful message in the best of economic times, and especially in today's challenging environment. The Phoenix calls.

I hope that my story and lessons from failure and success have offered some useful ideas and insights about dynamic entrepreneurship. It is not my aim to preach, but I would like to close with a few words of advice for students and supporters of entrepreneurship.

For students

When asked about career interests, European students are less likely than their American counterparts to put entrepreneurship on – let alone at the top of – their lists. That is changing, though. There is a "pull," from entrepreneurial success stories and more exposure to entrepreneurship at universities; and a "push," from traditional big company downsizing and reluctance to take on new hires.

So, my advice to students – first and foremost – is to be open-minded.

Think about alternative career paths. Take advantage of every opportunity to learn about entrepreneurship, through coursework and projects, interactions with entrepreneurs, and internships or summer jobs. Think broadly. There are opportunities in every industry, and in the public sector. Keep entrepreneurship in mind, not necessarily as a first job, but down the road a bit.

Before striking out on your own, I believe that it is valuable to gain some experience in a position with profit responsibilities (for a general management perspective, and a "buck stops here" feeling of accountability) ideally in an entrepreneurial setting (which can be a standalone enterprise or part of a larger company). Given the global nature of business, international experience is a huge plus, as well.

For academics

Entrepreneurship education has come a long way! But, there is still room for expansion and strengthening, especially in five areas: interactive methods, cross-disciplinary approaches, international networking, engagement of entrepreneurs, and tracking of student alumni. I'll briefly address each, in turn.

INTERACTIVE METHODS

Lecturing traditionally has been the main teaching method, at European universities. Entrepreneurship education calls for more experiential and action-oriented learning. Classroom teaching can benefit from case studies, which allow students to "see" a wide range of real entrepreneurs, and challenge them to figure out how to solve very real problems.

Field-based projects can be powerful learning experiences, especially when conducted in teams of students. Students and the community can both benefit when projects focus on a real business issue or opportunity, and involve interactions among students, and organizations and individuals in the community.

CROSS-DISCIPLINARY TEACHING

Entrepreneurship needs to be expanded across university campuses. The majority of entrepreneurship courses and professors are still business school-based. Bringing them to other areas – especially science and technology, the source of many innovations and new companies - is one approach. Creating incubators where students from a variety of disciplines can collaborate is another.

International networking

There is a tremendous opportunity to leverage knowledge and experience across national boundaries, both among academics, and between academia and the business community. Professors can participate in faculty exchange programs, attend international forums, and develop their own personal networks of contacts.

Engagement of entrepreneurs

Inviting entrepreneurs to be guest speakers is a good start, but just a start. Their value as role models and educators can be exponentially increased by entrepreneurship-in-residence programs that give them an active mentoring role. Entrepreneurs also can provide valuable input to curriculum design, and a source of new case studies.

Tracking of student alumni

What better source of engaged entrepreneurs than your own students! Few European universities currently track and reach out to their alumni, for financial and non-financial support. An understanding of students' post-university career paths also can inform curriculum development. Alumni also may be willing to be contacted by current students, for career advice and contacts.

For entrepreneurs

If you are an entrepreneur and skipped over the Chapter 7, please go back! It outlines a number of ways that you can give back to your university and your profession, and have a powerful impact on individual students. You can have an impact on your local community as well, by collaborating with local universities, and offering pro bono support to new entrepreneurial ventures.

On a broader level, you have the potential to create or support whole entrepreneurial ecosystems.

Take Hermann Hauser, for example. Born in Vienna, Austria, he is a successful IT entrepreneur, and contributor to Cambridge University's huge web of entrepreneurial spin-offs. He also was a major force behind the Hauser Forum, a state-of-the art focal point for entrepreneurship, designed to stimulate innovative collaboration between clusters of academics, start-up businesses and established industries.

For other institutions

There is a continuing need for attention to entrepreneurship education, on national and EU agendas. Progress is being made at the university level, but it must begin much earlier, at secondary and primary school levels. The goal of entrepreneurship education is not just job training. It is to plant seeds, to encourage attitudes and behaviours that will foster an entrepreneurial approach to work and life.

Much has been written about the barriers to entrepreneurship that plague Europe. There are structural issues to address, like labour mobility and penalties for business failures. But, equally important, we Europeans must continue to learn to accept and manage through language and cultural differences, within and beyond the region, to China and India and the world.

There is tremendous opportunity for entrepreneurs and entrepreneurship, in Europe. The Phoenix calls. I trust that we will all answer, in our own ways.

Acknowledgements

It is impossible to adequately thank all the people who have shared my entrepreneurial journey. I will make an effort here, with apologies in advance to anyone who I have inadvertently missed.

First and foremost, to my family.

To those who helped create this book.
Ken Freeman, Dick Latul, Tea Petrin, Shirley Spence, Karen Wilson

To all those who have taught and inspired me, contributed to Indivers' success, and helped promote entrepreneurship in Europe.

Jan Aalberts	Gerald Carter	Franklin Ewing	Daniel Isenberg
Derek Abell	Larry Clarckson	Joe Fitzpatrick	lie Isenberg
Punto Bawono	Kim Clark	Larry Fouraker	Pitch Johnson
Amar Bhide	Sandy Cesko	Ken Freeman	Roger Kollbrunner
David Birch	Pat Cloherty	Lucia Ganieva	Walter Kuemmerle
Jaap Blaak	Gordana Coric	Jack Glover	Dirk Kuin
Gabor Bojar	Tom Cummings	Philippe	Dick Latul
Peter Brooke	Marco Curavic	Haspeslagh	Tom Liebermann
Andrew Brown	George Doriot	Tim Healy	Rolf Liertz
Caroline le Brun	Bill Draper	Nada Hill-Spendal	Steve Marriotti
Art Buckland	Peter Drucker	Ove Hoegh	Gabriel Masfurolli
Roy Carriker	Hans Erkelens	Elizabeth Ingrassia	John McArthur

John McDonald

Jack McLean

Dan Muzyka

Heinrich von Molke

Yupar Myint

Klaus Nathusius

Pedro Nueno

Jos Peters

Tea Petrin

Peter Plasschaert

Julia Prats

John Quelch

Donna Rappacioli

Steve Ricci

Juan Roure

Bruno Roux de
   Bezieux

Tom Rurenga

Antonia Sariyska

Burckhard
   Schneider

Martin Schoeller

Victor Sedov

Neil Smith

Wim Stevens

William Stevens

Howard Stevenson

Jan Stolker

Parviz Tavakolly

Jeff Timmons

Ales Vahcic

Willy van der Luur

Leendert van Driel

Aad van Noord

Shai Vyakarman

Christine Volkman

Gordon Walsh

Christian Weinberger

Charlie Williams

Karen Wilson

Philip Yeo

Rinke Zonneveld

Author biographies

Bert Twaalfhoven, author

Bert was born in Holland. He earned his bachelor's degree from Fordham University, in New York City, and his MBA degree at Harvard Business School, in Boston. In 1993, he received an honorary doctorate from Fordham University, for his achievements in the area of education, and as an international entrepreneur. Bert is a former chairman of Harvard Business School Alumni, and received the 2001 Annual Alumni Award from HBS for his activities stimulating entrepreneurship in Eastern and Western Europe.

Bert founded and led Indivers B.V., a diversified multinational enterprise, for over forty years. Through Indivers, he started 65 companies in 14 countries including Italy, France, Germany, Russia, Ukraine, Holland, Belgium, England, U.S., Singapore and China. Bert also was a co-founder of the first venture capital company in the Netherlands (Gilde), and is involved in several venture capital firms.

Bert has been a passionate supporter of entrepreneurship throughout his career, giving over 260 talks to a variety of audiences, and playing an active role in international networks of universities and entrepreneurs. He is a co-founder and current president of the European Forum for Entrepreneurship Research (EFER). In its over 25 years of service, EFER has fostered and promoted research and teaching in the field of entrepreneurship at institutions of higher learning across Western and Eastern Europe.

Looking to the future, EFER aspires to broaden and deepen its support for entrepreneurship through faculty training and development, curriculum and course material development, and cross-border faculty collaboration and exchange. It also is actively working to engage business leaders and entrepreneurs, through its New European Champions and Entrepreneur-in-Residence initiatives, and an EFER Board of International Entrepreneurs.

Shirley Spence, co-author

Born in Montreal, Quebec, Shirley earned a bachelor's degree from Dartmouth College, in New Hampshire. Her early career included teaching high school French, and product management with Procter & Gamble Canada, after which she earned a master's degree in educational administration, planning and social policy from the Harvard Graduate School of Education, in Massachusetts.

The next portion of Shirley's career was spent as a management consultant. She became a partner at a firm that evolved into Oliver Wyman, based in Boston, MA. She specialized in organization system design and change management, working with a wide variety of companies in the U.S., Canada, Europe, and Africa. She also served the Boston Public Schools as a pro bono consultant. Shirley resigned from the firm several years ago, and continues to consult as a solo practitioner.

Shirley also spent several years at Harvard Business School, as a research associate. She has written over 50 print and multimedia case studies and teaching notes, and helped design curriculum for MBA courses and executive education programs. She assisted Howard Stevenson with a course called "Building a Business in the Context of a Life," and collaborated with him to write a book for philanthropic leaders called "Getting to Giving: Fundraising the Entrepreneurial Way, by a Billion-Dollar Fundraiser."

Index

Endorsements

"Bert Twaalfhoven is a legend in entrepreneurship! He exemplifies the values espoused in this "must read" for entrepreneurs and would- be entrepreneurs - LEARN, EARN, RETURN. Read all about it, and discover some of the ways to carry his philosophy to the next generation."

- Derek Abell, Founding President of the European School of Management and Technology (Berlin), and former Dean of IMEDE (Lausanne)

"This book makes many great points about entrepreneurship, and will teach future generations of entrepreneurs about giving back, to help make entrepreneurship a truly valuable and appreciated force in the betterment of our societies."

- Gabor Bojar, founder of Graphisoft and the Aquincum Institute of Technology (Hungary)

"Bert Twaalfhoven is a one man tornado. This book provides a personal and compelling introduction to how his philosophy of life - " Learn, Earn and Return" - allowed him to make major contributions, both as an entrepreneur and as a concerned citizen, while having enormous fun, and with his wife Maria, raising a family of eight children to be proud of. I am one of many who have been inspired by his example."

- Ken Freeman, former consultant, Interturbine; and Vice President and CFO, New Hill

"Learn Earn Return is a fantastic book for entrepreneurs at all stages and in all places. The candour of "16 failures, 50 million losses" is an invaluable source of practical wisdom. LER gives readers a real, no-holds-barred glimpse into the reality of entrepreneurship, without any window dressing."

- Daniel Isenberg, Professor of Entrepreneurship Practice, Babson Global

"LER reminded me why Bert was my first and most formative entrepreneurship mentor, shaping my thinking and behavior, as a re-entrepreneur. He also showed me how family and generosity can be important ingredients in business success. Hurray for BT, and 'the beat goes on' for entrepreneurs..."

- Tom Liebermann, former VP Business Development, Indivers; and Chairman and CEO, Advanced Systems International, Inc.

"Great book! LER offers real-life experience from a leading entrepreneur and major contributor to the development of entrepreneurship in Europe. Every student of entrepreneurship should read it."

- Juan Roure, Professor of Entrepreneurship at IESE, and co-founder of Europe's 500

"Bert's story is very inspirational for young people, as we are just starting our career and wondering if we have what it takes to be an entrepreneur. Each chapter opens a new horizon, and the stories and learnings from different places, industries and markets build an intriguing picture of the life of a real entrepreneur – filled with risks, failures, but also success and personal fulfillment."

- Antonia Sariyska, former President of JADE, a network of student-run businesses across 200 European universities

"Learn Earn Return" is a real treasure for any entrepreneur and entrepreneurship educator. The author's generous sharing of his life and entrepreneurship experience should help many young people to shape their entrepreneurial and life paths, and be really happy along the way."

- Victor Sedov, President and Board Member, Center for Entrepreneurship (CFE), Russia

"Bert Twaalfhoven is the epitome of an entrepreneur. His story is atypical only in that he has not only achieved in the business world, but also contributed to the education-

al realm. EFER has provided the spark that has ignited the entrepreneurial revolution among European business schools. Bert's vision of entrepreneurial education started before the wall fell in Berlin. His persistence has helped expose over 500 faculty members to the importance, the pedagogy, and the excitement of entrepreneurship."

- Howard Stevenson, Professor Emeritus, Harvard Business School

"Learn Earn Return offers thrilling insights into the personal and professional development, and the unique entrepreneurial achievement of a serial entrepreneur. I wish more entrepreneurs in Europe would follow Bert Twaalfhoven´s lead in his extraordinary commitment to entrepreneurship education!"

- Christine Volkmann, Chair of Entrepreneurship and Economic Development, Schumpeter School of Business and Economics, University of Wuppertal

"Bert Twaalfhoven is a prolific networker, and a passionate supporter of entrepreneurship. His perspectives are unique, imaginative, and have resulted in many successes. Useful lessons can be learned both from his success and his failures."

- Gordon Walsh, former CEO, Interturbine; and former President Business Unit, General Electric